Twayne's English Authors Series

Sylvia E. Bowman, *Editor*

INDIANA UNIVERSITY

Nicholas Udall

(TEAS) 30

NICHOLAS UDALL

by

WILLIAM L. EDGERTON

Nicholas Udall's play *Ralph Roister Doister,* generally regarded as the first complete English comedy, bridges the gap between classical and English drama, and he is seen in this study as one of the leading Protestant Humanists of the early Tudor period. Earlier appraisals of the famous play and of Udall have varied widely in completeness and accuracy; this study brings him into focus as an important literary figure and a leading exponent of the Humanist group.

The almost accidental character of the writing of *Ralph Roister Doister* is brought out in this close inspection of Udall's life. Far more important to him and to his contemporaries were other works he wrote in the role of Protestant Humanist—works long forgotten but deserving of attention in their own right. They are carefully considered in this study as works devoted to the pursuit of Humanism and the spread of Protestantism.

Nicholas Udall was a controversial figure in early Tudor England. There was much that could be frowned upon by the staunchest defender of his character. But he emerges here from scanty records and scattered sources as an understandable man, often misunderstood and unappreciated even in his own age.

Nicholas Udall

By WILLIAM L. EDGERTON

Howard University

Twayne Publishers, Inc.   ::   New York

For Gretchen

Preface

Nicholas Udall was not a great man, nor even a very good one; but his achievements were greater than literary histories give him credit for. Not only was he the first to unfold a story on the English stage with the attention to Classical structure and to that sentimental aspect of Terence that led to the romantic comedies of the Elizabethans, but he was also a Protestant humanist of considerable fame in his own day, and was long remembered after his death.[1] His first book, *Floures for Latine Spekynge* (1534), was used in schools for fifty years, probably even by Shakespeare, and it contains the seeds of *Roister Doister*. His *Apophthegmes* (1542) is a translation, with copious notes, of parts of Erasmus' *Apophthegemeta*, a compilation of sayings of the ancients; he had a major part in translating one of the best-known, if not most widely read books of the Elizabethan period, *The Paraphrase of Erasmus* (1549) (this was a collection of paraphrases of the "dark" parts of the New Testament); and his lost *Ezechias* was played after his death by Protestants for the special edification of their noncommittal Queen Elizabeth. Other books added to his fame, and his name appears in Roman Catholic indexes of prohibited books until 1900. Finally, by his personal friendships with his former students, who, in turn, became influential, he had an immeasurable, but certain effect on the course of education in the years that produced Shakespeare and his contemporaries.

The purpose of this study is to spell out Udall's achievements so that his *Roister Doister* will be seen to be the work of a scholar with a background that fitted him especially well for writing the first regular English comedy. His other achievements, also, need to be better understood, in order to see in focus what a typical Protestant humanist contributed to Tudor literature before re-

ligious strife ended that promising phase of literary history.
Further, it is time some more elaborate study of Udall is available
to students than they have had to get along with in the past.
Nowhere can they turn today to read an estimate of Nicholas
Udall that is as accurate as the accumulation of facts now war-
rants. This study is divided into two parts: first, a chronological
account of his life, touching on his publications only briefly; and,
second, a more detailed discussion of each of his major works.
Unless otherwise noted, I have modernized the spelling and
punctuation of Tudor English.

Several libraries have been helpful, among them the British
Museum; the Bodleian; the Folger Shakespeare; and libraries at
Duke, Harvard, North Carolina, Yale, and, especially, Pennsyl-
vania. Mr. John H. Harvey, Archivist to Winchester College, gave
generously of his time and knowledge, as did Mr. Maurice F.
Bond, Honorable Secretary to the Society of St. George's Chapel,
Windsor. Mr. Robert Birley, headmaster of Eton College, and Dr.
H. K. Prescott, the Eton librarian, also gave generous assistance.
Mrs. E. Cottrill and Miss D. Slatter, archivists at the Hampshire
County Record Office gave unstintingly of their expert knowledge,
as did Mr. Bruce Jones, borough archivist at Southampton. Wilkes
College helped make possible a summer's research at the British
Museum.

Naturally, my attempts to portray Udall rest on the work of
previous scholars whose knowledge of the man and his accomplishments have been of invaluable aid. From A. W. Reed I have
borrowed the simple method of trying, in this murky period, to
describe a man by reference to what others of his time said about
him. Although I differ with both of them occasionally, I owe much
—and more than is apparent by their mention in the notes—to
the work of G. Scheurweghs and T. W. Baldwin. Naturally, too,
the encouragement and the example afforded me by such men as
A. C. Baugh, Allan Chester, Matthew Black, and Matthias Shaaber
have been of the quiet, penetrating quality that have had an incalculable influence on what I have tried to do, although, also
naturally, none of these men can help it if a former student makes
mistakes.

WILLIAM L. EDGERTON

Howard University

Contents

Chronology

1504   Nicholas Udall born in Southampton during Christmas season. John Owdale, a town official, may have been father. Nicholas possibly related to Hampshire Uvedale family.

1517   Entered Winchester College. Immersed in Latin, including Terence; probably studied Greek.

1520   Entered Corpus Christi College, Oxford, the "beehive of humanism." Studied under Thomas Lupset and Vives; became friends with John Leland.

1524   Became Bachelor of Arts. Began lecturing to younger students as probationary fellow.

1526   Appointed full fellow and lecturer in logic and Greek.

1528   Involved in heresy hunt as a suspected Lutheran.

1529   Left Oxford at end of academic year.

1533   Wrote verses with John Leland for coronation of Anne Boleyn in May.

1534   February 28, dated Preface to *Floures for Latine Spekynge* from the Augustinian Friary in London.

1534   Appointed headmaster of Eton in June.

1534   July 13, created Master of Arts at Oxford.

1537   September 26, admitted Vicar of Braintree; held benefice *in absentia*.

1537   Sometime between October 12-24, probably produced *Thersites* at court.

1537   Received five pounds from Thomas Cromwell, presumably for playing at the court.

1541   Dismissed as headmaster at Eton in March.

1541   Wrote letter to unidentified patron in the spring admitting to wrongdoing in general terms. Probably went soon after to Carlisle.

1542   Udall's *Apophthegmes,* a translation of parts of Erasmus' *Apophthegemata,* published by Richard Grafton in September.

1543   Under patronage of Queen Catherine Parr, Udall became editor and chief translator of *The Paraphrase of Erasmus.*

1544   September 16, borrowed money to loan to friend; became involved in law suits as both creditor and debtor.

1545   Dated his Preface to Luke, in *The Paraphrase of Erasmus.* In Preface, Udall expressed thanks to Queen Catherine Parr for her patronage and declared his intention to translate other works for benefit of youth.

1546   March 30, shared with two others in the right of presentation to benefice of church at Hartyng, Sussex; sold rights shortly thereafter.

1546   June 10, borrowed ten pounds on promise to pay as soon as he was earning twenty pounds more a year than he was then receiving annually. Years of litigation followed.

1546   Sometime during this year probably wrote *Ezechias,* a Protestant propaganda play, now lost.

1547   Lived in precincts of Grey Friars; still there two years later.

1548   June 29, drew up report of controversial sermon preached at court by Stephen Gardiner.

1548   Praised highly by John Bale in catalogue of English writers. Bale attributed to Udall a translation of a play by Bernard Ochin, but the translation, if Bale was right, is now lost.

1548   Stephen Gardiner complained at *The Paraphrase of Erasmus* in letters from Tower of London in the fall.

1549   *The Paraphrase of Erasmus* published in January.

1549   Composed an answer to rebels of Cornwall, who objected to Protestant changes in church worship.

1549   Appointed tutor to Edward Courtenay, royal prisoner in Tower.

1550   Translated *Tractatie de Sacramente* by Peter Martyr, a Continental reformer. Udall's book, *A Discourse or Tractise of Petur Martyr,* was dedicated to Lord William Parr, brother of the late Queen Catherine Parr.

1550   July 13, granted valuable privilege to print books, including Bible.

1550 Gave evidence at trial of Stephen Gardiner in December.

1551 Contributed verses to two books of encomia: one published in memory of Martin Bucer, a Continental reformer; the other in memory of two sons of the Duchess of Suffolk, prominent patron of English Protestants.

1551 Appointed canon at Windsor December 14.

1552 Second edition of *The Paraphrase of Erasmus* published in January.

1552 Dated July 20 his preface to Thomas Gemini's *Compendiosa totius Anatomie delineatio*.

1552 *Roister Doister* probably produced at Windsor in the fall.

1553 First edition of Thomas Wilson's *Arte of Rhetorique* published in January; includes prefatory verse by Udall. In the same month, third edition of Wilson's *Rule of Reason* published; contains quotation from *Roister Doister*.

1553 April 26, Rector of Calborne, Isle of Wight.

1553 In July, Protestant Edward VI died, and Roman Catholic Mary Tudor ascended the throne.

1554 Arrested for non-payment of debt during Easter Term.

1554 June 20, Canonry at Windsor formerly held by Udall presented to Queen's chaplain.

1554 December 13, Queen Mary commanded Master of Revels to furnish Udall what he needed for presentation of play at court. Payments made to Udall between December 13, 1554, and January 5, 1555.

1555 November 12, bequeathed forty marks (about 30 pounds) by Stephen Gardiner.

1555 Appointed headmaster of Westminster School on December 16.

1556 Buried at St. Margaret's, Westminster on December 23.

CHAPTER 1

Early Days

I *Southampton*

NICHOLAS UDALL was born in Southampton during the Christmas season of 1504.[2] A "John Owdale" was the Southampton steward in 1505 and a baliff in later years, but since parish records were not kept in Southampton until the seventeenth century we cannot be sure if this man was the father, or even a relative, of the future scholar and playwright.[3] "Owdale" was a common variant spelling at the time for "Udall." Since "Uvedale" was also a common variant of "Udall," there has been a controversy for years about Udall's being connected with the prominent Hampshire family of Uvedale. A close relationship has been given credence in recent years by the discovery that a Thomas Uvedale (whose name in one record is spelled "Udall") lived near Winchester College while Nicholas Udall was there. Furthermore, some kind of relationship is suggested by tenuous connections with the Hampshire county family later in his career, but no definite conclusions can be made.[4]

Travelling companies of actors visited Southampton during Nicholas Udall's childhood, and it is therefore probable that he was familiar with the popular forms of drama before he went to Winchester College. If he had been the son of a town officer he would have had special exposure to drama, for travelling companies sometimes gave special performances before the local officials. But details of his early life come more into focus when we find his name mentioned on the admission rolls of Winchester College of 1517, where he is listed as being from Southampton and as twelve years old.[5]

II *Winchester College*

Winchester College in Udall's time, just as it is today, was no place for a dull or lazy student. Classes were held from seven until five, six days a week. Holidays and half-holidays were frequent, depending on the church calendar, but the longest vacation was the three weeks from Ascension Day (the Thursday forty days after Easter) to Corpus Christi (the Thursday after Trinity Sunday). Compared to today's schedules, the schoolboy's lot appears a hard one, but authorities differ about the actual time spent in studies by the pre-Reformation schoolboy. In general, however, Winchester schoolboys probably studied hard; for, as Arthur F. Leach puts it, "A chapter on the games and holidays of the boys might almost resemble that on snakes in Ireland." [6]

Latin, and not English, was the language not only of the schoolroom but of the entire school regime. A schoolboy in the public schools of Tudor England, particularly at this time, was immersed in Latin in a way that is difficult to conceive in these days of the preëminence of the vernacular. In fact, when laws were passed in Elizabeth's reign making the use of English obligatory in church services, the schools of Winchester, Eton, Oxford, and Cambridge were specifically exempt so that the students' education in Latin might not be weakened by the use of English.

Among the Latin authors that Udall would have become intimately acquainted with before he left Winchester would have been, among others, Virgil, Cicero, and especially Terence. Although Terence was probably not studied intensively until about Udall's third year at Winchester, Terentian phrases and sentences were the frequent basis for the "vulgars" that were part of his daily education in Latin all during his years at Winchester. "Vulgars" were English phrases and sentences with their Latin equivalents that were given the schoolboys to memorize in order to improve their use of Latin. Terence was especially favored as a basis for the "vulgars" by schoolmasters of the period because of his conversational qualities and the smoothness of his Latinity. Terence would have become an old friend to Udall by the time he left Winchester in 1520.

One of these collections of "vulgars" was written by William Horman, a former scholar, and later headmaster of Winchester just before Udall attended the school. *Vulgaria* (1519) reflects the life of the schoolboy at Winchester.[7] The sentences in the section "De Scholastica" are drawn from the boys' daily activities, and there seem to be none which does not correspond pretty closely with what we already know about the curriculum of the period. The only passages which do not seem to reflect a Spartan atmosphere are about plays and play acting. If these passages are based on subjects familiar to schoolboys—and there seems to be little reason to suppose otherwise—they reveal a far greater dramatic activity, or, at least, acquaintance with it, than is usually assumed of the grammar schools of the period.

The specific sentences in Horman's *Vulgaria* which refer to dramatic activity are as follows: "The apparel of this play cost me much money." "I will have made five stages or booths in the play. We lack players' garments, both for sad parts and mad." "I would have a place in the middle of the play, that I might see every pageant." "I am sent for to play well a part in a play." "I am principal player." "Who shall be players?" "I have played my part without any fail." "He put me out of the play." "Let us gather or make a shot or a stake for the minstrel's reward or wages." "I tarry for the minstrel, and him that should sing." "The minstrel did well his part; the bagpiper burst his bagpipe." "I delight to see interludes." "We have played a comedy of Greek; we have played a comedy of Latin."

Horman also includes many proverbs, which were characteristic not only of the contemporary interest in them, but also of Latin comedies. "It is an old said saw," Horman writes, with the Latin equivalent. "Though pepper be black it hath a good smack." "A given horse may not be looked in the teeth." "Wishers and woulders be small householders." Years later Udall was to have Merygreeke, the parasite in *Roister Doister*, begin the play with three "said saws" discharged in rapid succession.

The stress placed on both Latin and Greek in Winchester is reflected by Horman in these sentences: "Latin speech that was almost lost is now after long absence recovered and come again" (the distrust of medieval Latin by a Renaissance humanist is evident here). "Let young children be well taken heed of, that they learn no Latin but clean and fresh." "Lend me thy Tully, and thou shalt have him anon again." "Lend me thy Terence for this seven night." "Lend me thy Terence for my brother."

"It is no little point to undertake to write or speak Latin or Greek words convenient to the matter." "Tell me in Latin what he sayeth in Greek." "He uttereth goodly his Greek." "He applied himself with great diligence to Greek." "He hath founded a reader in Greek [a chair or professorship] for a hundred ducats a year." "I shall read openly a lecture of Greek if so be that honest wages be assigned out for the year."

Since so much that we know of Udall's early years is the result of adjusting the mirrors, as it were, of many separate investigations, it is obviously rewarding to have such a bright mirror as Horman's book. Unfortunately, however, records of dramatic performances at Winchester while Udall was there do not exist. Records of performances of school plays at other schools of the time do exist, however; and there was another activity at Winchester that may have had a bearing on the interest that Udall showed later in the drama: the festival of the Boy Bishop.

III *Festival of the Boy Bishop*

Vestiges of the rite of the Boy Bishop appear today in different parts of the world when, for one day of the year, usually during the Christmas season, social or professional status is turned upside down. Portions of the English army still set aside a day during the Christmas season when the ranks are reversed in various degrees of latitude, and traces of the ancient practice may still be seen in the American office party, where, for a few hours, "the Boss" becomes just another worker and hears from his employees how he ought to run his business. The Boy Bishop seems to have been the same kind of ceremony, when, in the words of the Winchester College Statutes of 1400, "We allow that on the Feast of the Innocents [December 28] the boys may say and perform vespers, matins and other divine services to be read or sung, according to the use and custom of the church of Sarum." [8] The celebration of the Boy Bishop apparently took place at other schools, and ecclesiastical establishments had a similar observance until the festival was abolished by royal proclamation in 1541. The Boy Bishop at Winchester was chosen from among the younger scholars on the eve, probably, of Innocents' Day. Although his episcopacy lasted only twenty-four hours, it was apparently absolute during this time.

The essentially dramatic nature of the Boy-Bishop ceremony has been summarized as follows: "The whole affair was a glorified masquerade. With these elements of the drama which exist in the assumption of disguises, in the recitation of prepared parts, in the serious pretence of being something which one was not, in losing for a time one's identity in that of a quite different person—with all these things the ceremony was replete."

As we have seen, Udall probably became acquainted with popular drama both at Southampton and Winchester. When he left Winchester for Corpus Christi College, Oxford, he had behind him four busy years in which he had learned to read and to write Latin as well as he did English. He had also almost certainly studied Greek. Further, he had been immersed in the plays of Terence—sometimes painfully, perhaps. He had at least seen, if not taken part in, the ceremony of the Boy Bishop. Many of the elements that were to make him later both a scholar and dramatist had already taken root.

CHAPTER 2

The Beehive of Humanism

I *From Student to Teacher*

CORPUS CHRISTI COLLEGE, Oxford, "the beehive of humanism," as it was called by the founder, Richard Foxe, was a new institution when Udall was admitted in 1520.[1] Specifically designed for the education of Humanists, it was for years regarded as one of the chief centers of Humanism in England. The founder counted among his personal friends such Humanists as Erasmus, More, and Linacre; and Corpus Christi College was hailed with enthusiasm by Erasmus. A revolt at Oxford against the teaching of Greek, during the year in which Corpus Christi first opened its doors, was settled in favor of the Humanists largely through the intervention of Sir Thomas More. Linacre sent Foxe a copy of his translation of Galen's *De Sanitate teunda,* in which he inserted a highly flattering compliment on the foundation of Corpus Christi. In short, Corpus Christi was a college especially close to the affections of Humanists as a foundation designed to further Humanistic studies.

It was a tiny college by modern standards—only fifty or sixty persons, including the faculty. About twenty students, called disciples, and twenty fellows, or professors, made up the nucleus of the college. There were also a few chaplains, clerks, and choristers and four to six sons of nobles or lawyers who were the predecessors of what afterward became known as gentlemen-commoners.

The regime imposed on the students was severe, and little time was allowed for any activity except studying. Only about twenty days a year were given students for vacation, and the faculty was allowed only about forty days. Except for the early versions of the gentlemen-commoners, mentioned above, the students were almost all what we would call scholarship students. They received what was in effect full tuition: a room within the college; board, including meals at noon and evening; and probably refections of a modest kind at other times; and clothing and tiny amounts of spending money. In many ways student life resembled that in a theological seminary, for strict observance of the canonical hours began at five in the morning. Members of the college slept only two in a room (although most Oxford colleges of the time were criticized for overcrowding)—a fellow in a high bed, and a student in a truckle bed. The fellow was generally responsible for the study and behavior of the student. According to statute only Greek or Latin could be spoken, and apparently this rule was followed carefully. Stimulus for foreign study, something like the modern foundation fellowships, was provided by encouraging one fellow at a time to take a three-year leave of absence in order to settle in Italy or in some other country for further study. He received his full allowance during his absence, and after his return he was to be available for the office of public lecturer when an opening became available.

The books the students studied, of course, were largely Classical as opposed to the conventional emphasis on medieval writers, but it was in the provision of public lecturers in both Latin and Greek, in addition to the usual lecturer in divinity, that Corpus Christi was revolutionary and most clearly Humanistic. In fact, the creation of the professorship in Greek seems to have been the first such permanent office created at either Oxford or Cambridge for the purpose of lecturing publicly, rather than privately, on the language and literature of ancient Greece. (Earlier, humanists like Grocyn or Linacre had lectured in Greek only in a private or a semi-public capacity). Further, the Greek lecturer seems to have been intended to be, as well as a Greek scholar, one of the principal officers of Corpus Christi.

In these Latin and Greek lectures, which seem to have been given for a short time by the same man during Udall's undergraduate years, we can see a direct link between two generations of Humanists. This man was Thomas Lupset. His lectures were popular, and he seems to have been eminently successful in carrying out the Humanistic purposes of the founder. His influence was of the kind that cannot be well described except in such clichés as "he instilled the love of humanism in his scholars." But it may be significant that Lupset—a friend and contemporary of such first-generation Humanists as More, Erasmus, Bude, *et al.*—should have lectured on Greek and Roman literature to men that can best be described as second-generation Humanists: John Leland, Richard Taverner, Richard Hyrde, Richard Moryson, and Nicholas Udall. Among other obvious marks of their Humanism is the fact that all, except Leland, translated parts of the work of Erasmus. If we were to look for a single link between these two generations of Humanists, we might well look no further than to the person of Thomas Lupset.

The second Greek lecturer seems to have been Edward Wotton, a fellow of Magdalen when he was lured to Corpus Christi by Foxe. The statutes of Magdalen College forbade his becoming a fellow of Corpus Christi; but he could be, and was, the lecturer in Latin and Greek. He is said to have been the first English physician to make a systematic study of natural history; and, although his accomplishments are too many and too specialized to be detailed here, the close acquaintanceship of this medical scientist with Udall may go far in explaining the success of Udall's editorial work for Gemini years later when he fitted a practical text to a series of scientific engravings for the use of surgeons.

The third Greek lecturer may have been Nicholas Udall. Wotton left to study medicine in Padua in 1524. In May, 1524, Udall received his Bachelor of Arts degree, and in September he became a *scholaris,* or probationary fellow. In 1526, after serving the required two years as a *scholaris,* he became a *socius,* or full fellow.[2] Between 1524, when Wotton left, and 1526, when Udall became a full fellow, no one was paid for teaching Greek, although Udall was paid for lecturing to younger students. But records show that Udall was paid for lecturing in Greek and logic in 1526-27 and in 1528-29.

Juan Luis Vives, the great Spanish Humanist, followed Lupset as a Latin lecturer in 1523. Although the exact dates of his lecturing are vague, he most probably lectured during the fall and winter of 1523-24 and again during the winter of 1524-25.[3] The influence of the educational thought of Vives—who insisted on the education of women, on special training of teachers, and on the importance of the vernacular—has often been pointed out, particularly in regard to Richard Mulcaster. But it is sometimes overlooked that Mulcaster was one of Udall's pupils at Eton and that, therefore, Udall was probably the connecting link between Vives and the important educational figure of Mulcaster.

It is true, of course, that Vives was no friend of the drama; in one place he writes of Plautus and Terence: "I should like to cast out of both of these writers all those parts which could taint the minds of boys with vices." But Udall's concern for moral purity is reflected in *Roister Doister*—one of the cleanest comedies in the sixteenth century. Furthermore, there is incalculable significance in the fact that Udall—whose career was spent largely in transferring to the vernacular the riches of Latin, and whose historical achievement was in writing, according to Latin principles, a vernacular play—did have the experience of attending the lectures and possibly conversing intimately with a Humanist who is remembered most for his insistence on the importance of the vernacular.

II   *The Heresy Hunt*

The gap in the record of payments for Udall's lecturing in Greek and logic during 1527-28, can be explained by showing that in that year Udall was involved in a heresy hunt at Oxford. According to the lengthy account of that episode in John Foxe's[4] *Actes and Monuments* (better known in the sixteenth century as the best-selling *Book of Martyrs*), a London curate was discovered to be supplying Oxford undergraduates with Lutheran works as well as the prohibited Tyndale translation of the New Testament. One of the Oxford men seized, an Anthony Dalaber, whose first-hand report is the basis of Foxe's account, mentions that among his "faithful bretheren and fellows in the Lord there" was the future author of *Roister Doister*.

However, in the correspondence arising out of the investigation several men are mentioned as ringleaders and Udall's name is not among them. The leaders seem to have been dealt with severely, but those not regarded as principals were let off with a good scare and with being forced to file past a bonfire and to cast into it their heretical books. In short, Udall was apparently one of the "multitude that be young and penitent and by other malicious persons seduced" who were dealt with, not by the crown, but by the college authorities. There seems little question that Udall, like many of the "most towardly young men in Oxford," as they were called, was naturally interested in the Lutheran movement, and in later years he was to be a strong supporter of the Reformation. But at this particular time, especially in such a stronghold of Erasmiasm as was Corpus Christi, his involvement seems to have stemmed more from intellectual curiosity than from religious zeal. Certainly he was not one of the leaders, and the following year he went back to his duties as a fellow at Corpus Christi.

III *Drama at Oxford*

Records of university performances at Oxford during the Tudor period contain not a single mention of Corpus Christi. However, there is a strong possibility that Udall wrote a play while he was at Oxford, perhaps for production at Magdalen College.[5] That play is *Thersites,* a faintly amusing little interlude based on a plotless dramatic dialogue which had been written in Latin hexameters by the French Humanist Ravisius Textor. *Thersites* has been regarded by one critic as a kind of rough sketch for the character of Ralph Roister Doister. A cowardly braggart, Thersites boasts of his prowess in battle, but is terrified by a snail; and, when challenged by a soldier, he runs away, dropping his sword and club.

Students of the play reinforce their conjecture that Udall was the author of *Thersites* by pointing to references by the author to places in Oxford and allusions to the same characters of English fiction and legend as appear later in *Roister Doister.* Udall himself refers to his attempts at writing while a student, presumably at Oxford. In his *Apopthegmes,* opposite a comment by Erasmus that Cicero once praised a man only for the exercise "to assay what I could do in a naughty matter," Udall wrote this marginal note:

Rhetoricians are wont for exercise to take feigned arguments of matters inopinable, and such are properly called declamations, and not orations. So did Homer write of the battle between the frogs and the mice and Erasmus wrote the praise of foolishness, another the praise of baldness, another of drunkenship: & this last argument I handled for my exercise, being a young student, albeit the same declamation now lies all worm eaten, as right worthy it is.   (325^r-25^v)

But whether or not future investigations substantiate conjecture about Udall's authorship of *Thersites,* compelling forces that finally resulted in *Roister Doister* can be descried in the exciting intellectual atmosphere of Humanism in which Udall was immersed while a student in the "beehive of English humanism" at Corpus Christi College, Oxford.

CHAPTER 3

Between Oxford and Eton

I   *The Silent Years*

UDALL left Oxford in 1529, but records are silent until 1533, when he turned up in London busy as both teacher and writer. Where he was during the intervening years is unknown for certain, but some reasonable conjectures can be made. When he applied for his Master's degree in June, 1534, he wrote that he had spent five years in study outside of Oxford. That period, of course, could refer partly to his vacations while he was attending Oxford, but some of that five years he obviously intended to be understood as having been spent in study after he left Oxford. It is true, of course, that he need not have attended any institution while studying outside of Oxford, but it is still tempting to speculate that he might have spent part of his time after leaving Oxford in studying at some German university. Under thinly disguised names, several of his countrymen did so at the time. A check of archives at Hamburg, where registers of students at universities during this period are preserved, has proved fruitless thus far, but that in itself is not wholly conclusive. Some of the registers are missing; moreover, Udall may have hidden his identity under an assumed name. Even now, perhaps, there may be hidden in a German clerk's imaginative spelling of his name (we have already seen what his countrymen could do to it) a record of Udall's attendance at Wittenberg or Tübingen.

Germany also was the place where school drama was thriving; and, although it is not necessary to assume so, it is still within the realm of possibility that Udall's strong interest in drama may have been stimulated in part by seeing what the German schoolmasters were doing. In fact, at some undefinable time in his career, probably around 1546, he wrote *Ezechias*, a play now lost and that has the same title as one of Sixt Birck's.[1]

All through the 1530's, Sixt Birck, the magister of the gymnasium of St. Anna in Augsburg, wrote plays, first in Latin for school performances, then in German for public performances. His plays had large casts in order to use as many boys as possible. William Gnaphaeus' *Acolastus* (a Latin play based on the theme of the Prodigal Son), which John Palsgrave was to translate so laboriously in 1540, had gone through its first three editions—1530, 1534, and 1536—before and during Udall's headmastership of Eton. Other Continental schoolmasters writing school plays at this time were, to mention only a few, Johannes Sapidus, at Strassburg; Sebastian Aerichaleus, at Prague; and Christian Hegendorfer. Latin and vernacular plays, written for schoolboys were commonplace on the Continent before and during Udall's Eton period (he was headmaster from 1534 to 1541). Although they were divided into acts and scenes, these Continental school plays did not reflect the dramatic structure or Terentian sentiment that one finds in *Roister Doister*.

But whether or not Udall spent the years between 1529 and 1533 in Germany, France or Italy (possibilities, because his work later suggests a knowledge of the language of those countries), he was certainly in London in 1533; for in that year he and John Leland wrote verses for the coronation of Queen Anne Boleyn.[2] The two men, whose coronation verses appear in the same manuscript, probably met several years before in Oxford. (Leland attended Oxford between 1522 and 1528, and one of his undated poems praises Udall's liberality when Leland was a poor scholar in need of money).

The strain of flowery hyperbole in their coronation verses has led one critic to accuse Udall of sycophancy, for in his representation of the Judgement of Paris he praises Anne Boleyn as being superior to the three goddesses. A modern criticism of "sycophancy" is probably inappropriate, however, for Leland's contributions are equally fulsome; and, as a matter of fact, flattery was conventional on occasions of this kind in the sixteenth century. In 1503 the daughter of Henry VII was welcomed at Edinburgh with a representation of the Judgement of Paris, and in 1584 George Peele repeated Udall's compliment by describing Queen Elizabeth as outshining the goddesses in his *Arraignment of Paris*. Further, Anne Boleyn's well-known Protestant leanings may have led Udall and Leland to be especially enthusiastic. There is probably considerable truth in the assertion, as one scholar has put it, that "this occasion was a much greater matter than a simple coronation pageant. It was the official recognition of the Revolt from the Papacy, and all who took part in it favored the new Faith." [3]

In addition to these possible reasons for the compliments of Udall and Leland, there may have been, if we can believe backstage gossip, still another reason for their extravagance of compliment.[4] The story goes, according to a prejudiced observer, Chapuys, the Spanish ambassador, that on the Easter Sunday before the coronation, a Dr. George Brown preached a sermon in Austin Friars in which, in accordance with a royal injunction, he urged the congregation to pray for the new queen. Most of the congregation left before the sermon was over—"murmuring and with ill looks." According to Chapuys, the king was much annoyed when he heard of it, and sent word to the mayor to see that nothing like that happened again. Thereupon, the lord mayor assembled the city companies and warned them not only that they must not murmur against the king's marriage, but also that they must prevent their apprentices, "and what is more difficult, their wives," from doing so. Granted that the story may be exaggerated, there still may be enough truth in it to allow us to picture the city fathers anxiously entreating John Leland and Nicholas Udall to be especially effusive in their expression of the city's joy and delight at being given such a wonderful new queen. Whatever posterity may think of the literary quality of these coronation verses (and, after all, they were intended only for a public pageant), there can be little doubt that their extravagant compliment and praise very much resemble an effort on the part of Leland and Udall to satisfy a group of worried city officials, anxious to have everything come off smoothly.

A sample of Udall's coronation verses follows. Anne Boleyn's entourage, which had landed at the Tower of London the day before, on the next day (May 31, 1533) made a ceremonial progress through the city to Westminster, stopping at shows and pageants along the way. These verses were part of a pageant at Cheapside.

Judgment of Paris

MERCURY

Jupiter this apple unto thee hath sent
Commanding in this cause to give true judgment.

PARIS

Jupiter a strange office hath give me,
To judge which is the fairest of these ladies three.

JUNO

All riches and kingdoms be at my behest;
Give me the apple, and thou shalt have the best.

PALLAS

Adjudge it to me, and for a kingdom
I shall give thee incomparable wisdom.

VENUS

Prefer me, and I shall reward thee, Paris,
With the fairest lady that on the earth is.

PARIS

I should break Jupiter's high commandant,
If I should for mede or reward give judgment.
Therefore, Lady Venus, before both these twin,
Your beauty much exceeding, by my sentence,
Shall win and have this apple. Yet to be plain,
Here is the fourth lady now in our presence,
Most worthy to have it of due congruence,
As peerless in riches, wit, and beauty,
Which are but sundry qualities in you three.
But for her worthiness, this apple of gold
Is too simple a reward a thousand fold.

The conclusion of this pageant is pronounced by a child:

No, no, another reward there is
Ordained for the worthiness of her grace,
And not to be disposed by you, Paris,
Nor to be given here in this place.
Queen Anne, most excellent that ever was,
For you is ready a Crown Imperial,
To your joy, honour, and glory immortal.
God, that of his goodness all things doth us send,

Hath sent us your Grace, our hearts to make glad.
Wherefore, with as much humbleness we intend
Your noble Grace to serve, as ever queen had.
For nothing there is that may now make us sad,
Having your noble Grace, our refuge and rest,
Provided by him, that knoweth what is best.

All joy, wealth, and honour, with long space of life
Be to your Grace, with succession royal.
And He that hath power of all prerogative,
The most blessed Trinity, God Eternal,
Save our King Henry in his estate royal!
Thus pray all the citizens, wife, child, and man,
God save King Henry, and his spouse Queen Anne.[5]

CHAPTER 4

The Eton Schoolmaster

I *Qualifications and Testimonies*

BUT if these coronation verses have little merit, a book published a year later (February, 1534) showed Udall to be a scholar of more than ordinary attainments. *Floures for Latine Spekynge* was designed to take the place of collections of "vulgars" (Horman's, quoted from earlier, is an example) by substituting the smooth conversational Latin of Terence for the textbook Latin of the schoolmasters. Although the chief aim of *Floures for Latine Spekynge,* as the title implies, was to improve the spoken Latin of schoolboys, it also furnished explanations of difficult constructions in Terence.[1] So well received was *Floures for Latine Spekynge* that it was used for fifty years by Tudor schoolboys. Its publication probably had a great deal to do with Udall's appointment a few months later (June 1534) to the position of headmaster of Eton.[2] This was a poorly paid but honorable post (only ten pounds a year) with exacting requirements, and the two preceding headmasters had later become bishops.

According to the Eton Statutes a headmaster had to have a Master of Arts degree, be unmarried, and be "a man of good character, skilled in grammar and teaching."[3] Udall received his Master of Arts degree at Oxford a month after his appointment to Eton. There is no record of his ever having been married. As for his character, it was obviously good enough to enable him to stay at Eton for nearly seven years, but it was weakness in his character that finally led to his downfall.

Udall's education at Winchester and Oxford guaranteed a thorough knowledge of Latin and Greek, and he had shown in *Floures for Latine Spekynge* that he had an exceptional understanding of the intricacies of Latin grammar and idiom. Further evidence of his learning, as well as an insight into how carefully he prepared for teaching has recently come to light with the discovery of a textbook bearing Udall's name and his many interlinear and marginal notes.[4] Thomas Linacre's *De Emendata Strvctura Latini Sermonis Libri Sex* (1525) is an advanced grammar text with many examples from classical literature of construction and syntax. The book is usually considered to have been too difficult for use in grammar schools. However, although Udall was teaching at Oxford when the book came out, and he placed "1525" after his name on the title-page, it is not clear that he used the book at Oxford. It appears rather to be the kind of book a zealous Eton headmaster would at least try out on his pupils, or refer to in teaching. Udall went through the book carefully and annotated parts of it heavily, with corrections of misprints, exact indications of sources of quotations, and many translations of the Greek phrases and sentences into Latin.

One way of judging a schoolmaster's skill in teaching is to find out what his students thought of him in later years and what successes in life they later achieved. A well-known complaint about Udall by a former student appeared in Thomas Tusser's *Fiue Hundreth Points of Good Husbandry* (1573):

> From Paul's I went, to Eton sent,
> To learn straightways the Latin phrase;
> Where fifty-three stripes given to me at once I had
> For fault but small, or none at all.
> See, Udall, see, the mercy of thee, to me, poor lad.
> (II, 27ᵛ)

Since this doggerel appeared in nearly twenty editions up to 1638, it is likely that Udall's reputation as a flogger was known to thousands. Such a reputation, however, would not necessarily have been held against him in the sixteenth century; stern discipline, including beatings, was common throughout the sixteenth century as a means of making reluctant schoolboys learn their Latin. Readers of Roger Ascham's *The Schoolmaster* will remember with what approval Walter Hadden remarks that he had studied under "the best schoolmaster and the greatest beater." (Hadden's remark used to be thought to refer to Udall, but we now know he was referring to Richard Cox).

A less painful testimony to Udall's teaching than Tusser's, but not so well known, is that of John Parkhurst, Bishop of Norwich, who wrote this tribute to his former teacher:

> You understand Greek and Latin letters
> And you teach them truthfully.
> The natural disposition of your talent, Udall,
> Is to make them full of life.
> You make to spirits, wanting and striving,
> A present of the gods.
> These things you do because, Udall, you unite in yourself
> A genuine love for them.[5]

Perhaps it was in part the admiration for a former teacher that led men who had once studied under Udall at Eton to choose his play *Ezechias* to put on before the Queen when she visited Cambridge in 1563. And although we cannot at this distance in time be wholly fair and complete in listing all his students who achieved eminence in later life, we can, at least, note a few whom any schoolmaster would have been proud to have taught.

For example, Thomas Wilson's name will appear frequently in this account of Udall's life as a close friend and one whose name is bound up closely with the composition of *Roister Doister*. He achieved fame as both author and statesman. In addition to writing the influential *Arte of Rhetorike* and *The Rule of Reason*, he wrote a tract on usury of great significance for historians; and he climaxed a successful legal career by becoming a secretary of State under Queen Elizabeth. Another former student of Udall's, the noted Richard Mulcaster, mentioned earlier as an important educational figure, became headmaster of the Merchant Taylor's School, where he taught Edmund Spenser, Thomas Kyd, and others, and often took his boys to court to perform in plays before Queen Elizabeth. Professor Baldwin even traces an interesting connection between Udall and Shakespeare by demonstrating that Thomas Jenkins (almost certainly one of Shakespeare's teachers) probably attended the Merchant Taylor's School under Mulcaster.[6] Naturally, of course, it is impossible to define exactly the intangible influences that a teacher has on his students; in fact, it can be argued that some men achieve eminence despite their teachers. It seems also clear that Udall's greatest influence on later generations was through his writings, as we shall see when we examine his books in more detail. Nevertheless, it is probably not too much to say that Udall's influence as a teacher, despite his downfall at the end of his career at Eton, was that of a Humanist who handed on to his students that respect for learning and letters that had so much to do with the greatness of Tudor literature.

II *Drama at Eton*

Unfortunately, incomplete records at Eton contain no mention of dramatic productions during Udall's tenure as headmaster. It is possible, nevertheless, that Udall may have been active in fostering drama at Eton. From his own experience at Winchester, he would have been aware of the dramatic possibilities of the rites of the Boy Bishop. It is possible, too, that he was well aware of the activities of German schoolmasters. Almost certainly he took time out from his teaching to put on a play at court in the fall of 1537. The play is *Thersites,* referred to earlier as probably having been written by Udall while he was at Oxford.

The surviving version of the play contains a prayer at the end that shows it was put on at court between October 12 and October 24, 1537. An account book of Thomas Cromwell's includes the following note: "Woodall the scolemaster of Eton—The seconde of ffebruary gyven to hym by my Lordes commaundement for pleing byfore hym v^{li}." [7] The date in the account book is usually taken to be February, 1537; and that date, of course, means the "pleing byfore hym" refers to a date earlier than the fall of 1537. If however, the date is really February, 1538, then the payment might refer to *Thersites.* At the very least, we have evidence that Udall appeared at court in one year or the other. Further, on September 26, 1537, Udall was appointed vicar of Braintree, a post of modest income, but one which he served *in absentia,* for he was relieved of the duty of residence the following year by royal dispensation. And finally, a letter by Robert Aldridge, Provost of Eton and Bishop of Carlisle, that mentions "Mr. Udall, late Scholemastre wose Roome nowe enioeth and occupieth Mr. Tyndall, your owne true scholere and bedman" can be dated October 1537. The story is a complicated one, but the implication is clear: Udall was temporarily absent from Eton during the period he could have produced *Thersites* at court.[8]

The Eton Schoolmaster

Twenty years after Udall left Eton, a former student, then the headmaster of Eton himself, wrote that it was an established custom at Eton for the school to put on a play during the Christmas season. A play was selected around the feast of St. Andrew (November 30) "according to the schoolmaster's choice, which seems best and most appropriate to him, which the boys may act, not without the elegance of Roman plays, before a popular audience sometime during the Christmas season. Occasionally he may also present dramas composed in the English tongue which have cleverness and wit." [9] It is purest speculation, of course, but it is possible that *Thersites* may have been put on at Eton, where it was seen by courtiers from Windsor, not far away, who later saw to its presentation at Hampton Court during the birth festivities of Edward VI.

Thomas Wilson catalogued amusingly in *The Arte of Rhetorike* —written while he was in close association with his former teacher—the faults which Udall may have attempted through school plays to eliminate from his flock:

Pronounciation stands partly in fashioning the tongue, and partly in framing the gesture . . . One pipes out his words so small, through default of his windpipe, that you would think he whistled. Another is hoarse in his throat, so that a man would think he came lately from scouring harness. Another speaks as though he had plums in his mouth. Another speaks in his throat, as though a good ale crumb stuck fast. Another rattles his words. Another chops his words. Another speaks as though his words had need to be heaved out with levers. . . . Another barks out his English Northern-like, with "I say!" and "Thou, lad!" Another speaks so finely as though he were brought up in a lady's chamber. Some speak as though they should tell in their sleeves. Some cry out loud, that they would make a man's ears ache to hear them.

Some cannot speak but that they must go up and down, or at least be stirring their feet, as though they stood in a cockering boat. Another will play with his cap in his hand, and so tell his tale . . . Some pore upon the ground as though they sought for pins . . . Some talk as though their tongues went upon patines . . . There are a thousand such faults among men, both in their speech and in their gesture, the which, if in their younger years they be not remedied, they will hardly be forgot when they come to man's state.[10]

III *Signs of Weakness*

But to turn from Udall's achievements at Eton to a less pleasant aspect of that period: On March 9, 1536, he signed a bond undertaking to pay Henry Crede, a clothman of Wilton, on the following Easter the sum of twenty pounds.[11] Since this was the equivalent of two years' salary as headmaster, it would be interesting to know what other income or assets Udall had at this time. His income from *Floures for Latine Spekynge* may have been considerable, of course, and in our discussion of *Thersites* we have seen that he was in favor at court during this period. He may, for example, have had foreknowledge of his appointment in September, 1537, to the rectory of Braintree, or to some other living. In any case, Udall failed to pay the debt, and the case was carried on in law courts for years. He was "outlawed" in the City of London on November 25, 1538, for non-payment.[12] In 1544 Udall declared in court that he had paid the debt in Cornwall. In 1545 a Cornwall jury turned in a verdict against him, and he finally gave satisfaction to Crede and took advantage of the Act of General Pardon of 1544 to have his outlawry pardoned. Although the term "outlawry" today among laymen conjures up images of masked cowboys, in the sixteenth century the term was used to describe a common civil action brought against a defendant for, among other things, non-appearance at court in cases of misdemeanor. Such non-appearance seems to have been at issue here, for Udall insisted that he had paid his debt outside the City of London. It is hard to discover from this distance of time what the case really amounted to. It has often been observed that the sixteenth century was a litigious age, but, on the face of it, Udall clearly was in the wrong. Later on in his career Udall was in lawsuits several times, but less censure springs to mind then than in this first evidence of a weakness in Udall's character. As an Eton headmaster he would have been expected as a matter of course to be above reproach, but the fact that he was not is clear, not only in this case but in an even more damaging accusation in March, 1541.

CHAPTER 5

A Turning Point

I *On Trial Before the Privy Council*

IN March, 1541, Udall's career as the headmaster of Eton came to an abrupt end. He was charged with a serious crime before the Privy Council and sent to the Marshalsea. At the same time he wrote an abject letter to his patron confessing, if not to the crime, at least to a period of dissolute living which he could not defend. And yet, despite this calamity, Udall's career as a scholar-translator, interrupted for eight years since the publication of *Floures for Latine Spekynge,* became brighter than ever after his dismissal from Eton. How, then, can we reconcile the attitude of Udall's friends with the following words in the Privy Council register?

The evidence, taken at face value, is enough to end any man's career. On the 12th of March, 1541, according to the Privy Council Register, "John Hoorde, late scolar of Eton, examined of a certain robbery surmised to have been done at Eton by the sayde Hoorde & others, and confessing the fact, as apperith by his confession in writing, was committed to the keping of the clerk of the check of the guard." [1] On the same day, William Emlar, goldsmith of London, was committed to the porter's ward "for the buying of certain images of silver and other plate which was stolen from the college of Eton." The next day, March 13, Thomas Cheyney, "late scoler of Eton," made a confession similar to Hoorde's and was also taken into custody.

The following day, on March 14, "Nic. Vuedale, Scoolmaster of Eton, beying sent for as suspect to be of councail of a robbery lately commited at Eton by Thomas Cheyney, John Hoorde, Scolers of the sayd scole, and . . . Gregory, seruant to the said scolemaster, and hauing certain interrogatoryes ministred vnto hym, toching the sayd fact and other felonious trespasses, wherof he was suspected, did confesse that he did commit buggery with the said cheney, sundry times heretofore, and of late the vjth day of this present moneth in the present yere at London, whervpon he was commited to the marshalsey." A few days later the fathers of the two scholars appeared before the council and were put on recognizance to appear with their sons for a further hearing. Emler, the goldsmith, was also called in again and put on recognizance to appear at some future date within a year, and that is the last we hear of the case in the minutes of the Privy Council.

On the face of it, the record seems clearly to convict Udall of the grossest immorality. There is no question but that buggery, in 1541, was considered a heinous offence. An Act of Parliament in 1533-34 declared that "since there is not yet sufficient punishment . . . buggery shall be adjudged a felony, (and) offenders shall suffre such paynes of deth losses and penalties as felons byn accustomen to doo." The act was continued in the next Parliament in 1536; again in 1539; and in 1540 the act was extended to cover persons in holy orders and was made "eternal." [2]

If we knew nothing of Udall's later career, we would have no reason to suspect that the case was any different from the way it appears on the record. And yet, as A. W. Reed has pointed out, "there is no doubt that Udall had lost neither the confidence of his friends nor ultimately that of the Privy Council." [3] But some scholars have disregarded this paradoxical situation and have taken the evidence in the Privy Council register at its face value. Typical of these judgments are such statements as "his manner of life was not such as to render him an ornament to any religious party." Other scholars have referred to "his recent transgressions," or they have described him as a man of "unsavory character." [4]

As a matter of fact, the obvious conclusion that comes to mind if we view the case dispassionately is that Udall had powerful friends at court or on the Privy Council who kept his offenses and trial secret. Thomas Wriothesley, who, it has been suggested, may have been Udall's patron at the time, was on the Privy Council and attended the meeting when Udall's case was heard. Keeping the whole matter secret would help explain the paradox of Udall's apparently undamaged future career as a scholar. This theory, however, leaves unexplained not only the Council's leaning over backward later to befriend Udall, but also why, if it was so anxious to keep the matter secret, it allowed his case to become a matter of record in the first place. (Historians are only too aware that the Privy Council included in the register only matters it felt like recording).

This willingness of the Council to record the hearing becomes even more puzzling when we realize that Thomas Cheyney, the scholar involved in Udall's confession, was probably a relative by marriage of Thomas Wriothesley.[5] Cheyney's father is described in the Council register of March 15 as "Robert Cheyney de Chessamboys in Com Buck, armiger [knight]." Wriothesley's wife, according to the *Dictionary of National Biography*, was a daughter of William Cheyney, also of Chesam Bois, Buckingham. This relationship, added to the possible connection of patron to Udall, would have led Wriothesley, if the offense had really been buggery, to have made certain that the affair did not leak outside the close circle of the Privy Council, or, at least, to see that it was not made a matter of record.

We are still left to assume that such a confession as Udall made could have been kept from being a matter of common report in court circles by even the most powerful of government officials, and Wriothesley, of course, had his share of enemies; and we are still confronted with the puzzle of the benefits which Udall received subsequently, not only from royalty, but even from the Privy Council itself.

There is one solution, although it means cutting the Gordian knot, and that is to suppose that an error was made in recording Udall's confession in the Council register. According to E. R. Adair, who made a close study of the Privy Council registers, the procedure followed in keeping the register at the time of Udall's appearance before the Council was one which might well have allowed errors to enter the record.[6] The Clerk of the Council, who at this time was William Paget, took rough notes during the Council meeting; and later, these, together with "the letters that the council dispatched, the recognizances, the appearances, and the other miscellaneous matter, were entered in a book from day to day. Paget started with every intention of keeping his register in beautiful order," continues Adair, "but it is almost amusing to see, in the deterioration of the handwriting, how pressure of business forced him to be content with making the entries as rapidly as possible."

If Paget were working under such pressure as his entries indicate and if indeed his handwriting were deteriorating in the way Adair describes it, it is not at all impossible to assume that, simple as it may sound, we have the answer to the enigma before us. "Buggery" and "burglary" are near enough alike, especially if written in rough notes by a hurried clerk, to be mistaken for each other. In the rapid transcription of rough notes, a clerical error is not at all impossible. Further, a blank clearly exists where a word has been left out in the register just before Gregory's name.[7] This suggests that the rough notes for this entry may have been hopelessly illegible at this point.

Not only is "burglary" near enough to "buggery" to be mistaken for it, but it fits into the case the Council was considering more logically. The Council's chief concern seems to have been with the robbery of church ornaments at Eton. According to the *New English Dictionary*, in 1541, "burglours" were "properly such as feloniously in ye time of peace brake any house, church, etc." The robberies at Eton may have consisted in the drunken headmaster's breaking open the chests containing the church ornaments and of giving them to the boys to sell to the goldsmith. If that is so, Udall might have in this case extended their operations to London. The logical confession that the Council would hope to get from the headmaster would be one that would serve to convict him of burglary. Ten years later the canons of Windsor were investigated about the disappearance of church property. Their defense was simply that they believed they had a right to it.

Any attempt to whitewash Udall's character at this period in his life is useless, for he stands condemned in his own words. There can be no doubt, however, that a period of dissolute living—ending, perhaps, with drunken traffic in church goods—was misbehavior which the patron of a brilliant scholar would be glad to overlook after he had reformed his life completely. Too many people had misappropriated church property at that time to make it seem the heinous crime it appears to us. Seen in this light, the following letter Udall wrote at the time of his Council appearance appears to be, although an abject confession of wrongdoing, not the kind of letter he would have written if his offense had been unforgiveable.[8]

II *A Letter of Remorse*

Right Worshipfull and My Singular Good Master

Although I perceive your labour for my restitution to the room of schoolmaster in Eton not to have taken such effect as your mastership's good will was, yet do I (as I am most bound to do) for your great travail, pains, and trouble in that behalf sustained, render no less thanks than if it had succeeded and come to pass according to my request and your mastership's expectation. And having your mastership's favour I am and shall be as well contented that my suit had not taken place as I would have been glad to have recovered that room, which I was never desirous to obtain but only of an honest purpose to discharge my debts and by little and little as I might to pay every man his own, most humbly beseeching your mastership to extend your benign favour towards that purpose, and of your abundant pity to set your helping hand to the bestowing of me to such condition where I may by sober living be recovered to some state of an honest man.

Let not despair so deeply enter into your most gentle heart to think me past amendment, but rather call to mind that Plinus says: *tum demum praecipuam esse cloementiae laudem, cum irae caussa iustissima est* [the chief value of mercy lies precisely in the fact that the cause for anger is most just]. He needs no mercy nor forgiveness who has not offended. *Et quis tandem mortalium sapit horis omnibus? Imo (quod ait poeta)*

Si quoties peccant homines sua fulmina mittat
Juppiter, exiguo tempore inermis erit.

[And who among the mortals is judicious all the time? Nay, rather (as the poet says) if Jupiter hurls his thunderbolts as many times as men err, in a short time he will be without weapons].

What servant has not continual need of the clemency of his master? For my part, as I cannot excuse myself but that I have deserved your displeasure and indignation, so I trust my offenses *humana quidem esse et emendari* [as they are indeed human they can be corrected]. And if pity and compassion may move you to receive me to your grace and favour, I trust you shall find that this your correction shall be a sufficient scourge to make me, during my life, more wise and more aware utterly for ever to eschew and avoid all kinds of all manner of excesses and abuses that have been reported to reign in me. For the love of Christ, consider in what extremity and distress I am constitute. Consider that if you should reject me and cast me off, though I were in no man's danger, yet no man of honour or honesty will either receive me, or do for me, or favour, or look upon me. Consider that, forgoing your favour, I shall therewith lose *amicos, fortunas, spesque omnes, existimationem denique ac vitam* [friends, fortune, and all hope; in short, reputation and life], nor live six days out of prison; all which things (I trust to your heart's rejoicing in time to come) only your goodness may save and redress.

Since the time that your mastership at the intercession of my good friends promised upon my honest demeanor from thenceforth to be my good master, to my knowledge I have not eftsoon offended. And in what heaviness, in what sorrow, in what pensiveness of heart I have lived since coming from Titchfield, though I were able to express (as indeed no man is) it would be to your mastership incredible. No sickness, no loss of worldly goods, no imprisoning, no torments, no death, no other kind of misfortune could have pierced my heart or made in it so deep a wound as has this your displeasure, which wound, if it might please your goodness with the salve of your merciful compassion to bring for this one time *ad cicatricem* [to the wound] you should not need in all your life again to fear *ne quando mea culpa vitioque recrudesceret* [lest my error and moral failing break out again].

Be good, master, to me this once. If ever I shall be found again to offend in any such kind of transgressions as at this time has provoked and accended kindled your indignation against me, I shall not only be my own judge to be accounted forever most unworthy the favour and goodwill, either of your mastership or of any other honest friend, but also to be most extremely punished to the example of all others. οὐ γὰρ ἀγνοήσεις αὖθις ἔνθα δ χαύχασός ἐστιν, οὐδ' ἀπορήσεις δεσμῶν ἤν τι τεχνάσων ἁλίσχωμαι,
vt ait Lucianicus ille prometheus [for you will not forget again where the Caucasus is, nor will you want for chains if I am caught scheming anything, as Lucian says in his Prometheus].

Though I be not worthy to receive any favor at the hands of your mastership, yet is your excellent heart and noble stomach worthy to show favor. And like as it cannot be chosen but that the more tenderly your mastership has favored and loved me, the more grievously the same must take my lewdness and folly, even so can I not despair but that the more hatred of vices that is rooted in your most honest and heroical heart, the more propense [inclined] the same is to show mercy and forgiveness to all such as with whole heart and purpose of amendment without dissimulation return to the wholesome path of honesty from which by youth or frailty they have chanced for a time to swerve. I cannot persuade myself that your mastership hates anything in me or anyone else anything except vices. Neither can I any other think or judge than all this severity towards me to have proceded of your most tender zeal and good mind, only of purpose to have my folly redressed. Which effect, if you were certain thereof might ensue (as I trust in God you shall find it) I have conceived that hope of your goodness that you would rather my person to be saved than spoiled, rather to be reformed than destroyed, rather to amende than perish.

All vices of which I have been noted or to your mastership accused, being once by the roots extirpated, and in their places the contrary virtues with constant purpose of good continuance in the same deeply planted, I trust you would become better master to me after my amending and reformation than if I had never in such wise transgressed. And forasmuch as experiments hereof cannot be had without proof, it may please your mastership to use towards me some moderation and in this to follow the good fashion of an indulgent and tender parent *qui delinquentibus liberis non ante extrema supplicia admouet, quam remedia consumperit* [who would not apply extreme punishment, which would destroy any hope of cure, for failings due to freedom from restraint].

If it may please your goodness to forget what is past χαὶ δευτερων μεινόνων *quod Graeci dicunt* [my subsequent conduct being improved, as the Greeks say] to prove me once again, I doubt not by God's grace so honestly to redub all things that I will (God helping) give you more cause to be glad of me than ever you had to take displeasure with me. And I doubt not but that it shall more rebound to your worship, by your clemency to have made of an unthrift an honest man, than through your extreme severity to suffer me utterly to be cast away. To hurt, to undo, to spoil a man is a thing of small glory and easy for every man to do, but to preserve or to recover a man from present extinction *hoc demum magni excelsique ac generosi est animi* [that and that alone is the soul of greatness and nobility].

The Greek and Roman histories are full of the immortal laud, glory, and commendation of such as in cases like to this have instead of rigor and severity used such moderation of mind, such lenitee [mildness], such gentleness and clemency, that they have thereby won to goodness innumerable persons which by extremity of rigor must needs utterly have been lost.[9]

Nec est, vti confido, vsqueadeo perdita vita mea, quin tua bonitate ad frugem reuocari atque reduci queam, nec adeo deplorata vt nullus ne spei quidem locus relinquatur [Nor is my life, I trust, so far abandoned in every respect that you may not rescue it by goodness, and thus save it, nor is it to be regarded as having reached a point of dissoluteness beyond all hope of recovery]. Scipio Africanus the Elder (to whom the gentle histories do attribute this honorable testimony, that the gods immortal wanted him to be born into this world that there might be some man in whom virtue, goodness, and honesty should in all points singularly excell, pass, and show itself) is by the self-same history, mentioned to had been of a very riotous and dissolute sort of living in his youth, and the rather thereby to have grown afterward to the much more excellency of all virtues in the rest of his time, when he had once shaken off that impotency of voluptuous appetites.

It is also read of C. Valerius Flaccus that he was in youth a famous example of all riotousness, and the same, when he had in process of time converted his life to the contrary, became an example of all frugality, religion, sobriety, and holiness, infinitely more wholesome and profitable to the commonwele than he had afore been pernicious in the same. No man at those days lived in more slander and infamy than did Q. Fabius Maximus being a young man, or, after his conversion and changing of life, any man for honesty, wisdom, and gravity with the same Fabius worthy to be compared.

One Polemon of Athens, a philosopher, a man in his youth not only drowned in voluptuousness, but also setting his most delight and felicity in the very infamy of the same, newly arisen from banqueting and reveling, not in the evening after sunset, but in the morning, after sunrising, and espying the door of Zenocrates' school open, resorted thither drunken as he was, willfully to disturb not only the said Zenocrates then reading a public lecture in philosophy, but also all his auditory [audience], Zenocrates, not changing countenance at his coming in, but altering the matter of his reading, began somewhat to declare of the feditee [foulness] of riot and drunkenness and of the comeliness of sobriety. Which, Polemon hearing, was suddenly converted and from thenceforth became a philosopher of singular gravity, of incomparable soberness, of most constant virtuousness, and so continued all his life after.

If these persons and others innumerable of like sort had been taken at the worst, neither they had aspired to those degrees of most laudable honesty and virtue, nor such [persons] as saved them from the perils and dangers thereof and by their great tolerancy brought them to goodness, had purchased that prease [praise] to their immortal glory. Let these examples somewhat move your mastership to pity and compassion for that that is past, and to hope that I may ere now be amended for the time to come.

That if you can entreate your most gentle heart not to be inexorable nor inflexible towards me your poor servant, no less minding than to make full amendes for all that in time past has been amiss, for His sake, that of His infinite mercy forgave and daily still forgives to us, being most unworthy, all our offenses and casts them behind His back never after to entwite [rebuke] or to remember them again, be for this one time pitifull towards me, who by your mercy may be recovered, and by your indignation must needs perish forever.

Hear and accept this my most piteous lamentation proceeding from the bottom of my heart, being most sorrowful that it should be my chance to incur your indignation. Accept this mine honest change from vice to virtue, from prodigality to frugal living, from negligence of teaching to assiduity, from play to study, from lightness to gravity. Nor esteem it the worse or the lighter from that it begins of repentance, but rather persuade yourself that the same repentance shall still remain within my breast as a continual spur or thorn to prick and to quicken me to goodness from time to time as often as need shall require. And that you think not that I mean any worse or any less to prove mine honest manner of living, and to content and satisfy the minds of all such as upon any occasion have conceived any ill opinion of me, I shall not require of your mastership anything but only that without which no man can live and which shall please your mastership to allow me as you see cause and none otherwise: beseeching the same, if you possibly may, to forget that is past and cannot now be again undone, and once again to take experiment of me, and as you shall find me, so to use me, considering always that as another besides may happen to do amiss, so may I as well as another amend.

And where percase [by chance] *aeris alieni magnitudo animum tuum deterret* [the size of my debts may cause you misgiving] I doubt not, having your mastership's favor and good help, to be able to shake it off within two or three years at the uttermost by such means as I shall declare unto your mastership if it may please the same to hear me and help me, whereby I shall be (as I am already) most bounden to pray to God to preserve and continue your good mastership long in health and prosperity.

Your most bounden orator
and servant   Nicolas Udall

Since this letter is obviously significant in the career of the author of *Roister Doister*, certain important questions arise. To whom was the letter addressed? What does the letter tell us about the nature of Udall's offense? Is the letter a sincere expression of remorse and promise of reform? If so, did it have its effect?

Udall mentions that he has lately come from Titchfield, and, chiefly on the basis of that mention, it has been assumed that

Wriothesley was his "most singular good master," or patron, at this crucial moment in his life.[10] However, it is possible that any one of three other men could have been his patron: John Udall, Robert Aldridge, or Richard Cox. John Udall was high in court circles and may have been a relative, and Aldridge and Cox were Eton headmasters themselves who were then in positions of influence.

Unfortunately, no matter how carefully we read the letter, we can come to no definite conclusion about the nature of Udall's offense. He obviously admits to having disgraced himself and his friends; he does not try to say that he has not been guilty of something, and that, too, pretty serious. But the general impression he tries to create is that the offense, serious as it is, is a folly of youth who is capable of reform. Since his references to his offense do not rule out buggery, for he asserts that he could not live outside of prison six days without the help of a patron, neither does his description rule out some lesser offense; for any disgrace at all reflecting on his character could have been disastrous to his career. Notice, too, that the offense, whatever it was, did not prevent both him and his patron from trying to get back his post at Eton, a fact which suggests that his crime could not have been of a heinous moral character.

Although the letter is unclear about the offense, it does show Udall to have been sincere in his remorse and in his promises of reform. Some of the sentences, with their cries from the heart, have the tone of sincerity we associate with genuine repentance at any time. Perhaps an echo of the whole incident is reflected in a note that he wrote the following year on the subject of repentance in his *Apophthegmes* (342). After a statement by Demosthenes that he would not give ten thousand drachmas to stay one night with Laïs, for "I will not buy repentance so dear," Erasmus had noted: "Unto unhonest pleasure, repentance is a prest [ready] companion." Adds Udall: "Yea, and one property more it hath, that the pleasure is small and is gone in a moment; the repentance great, and still enduring as long as life continueth."

Perhaps to modern ears certain characteristics of the letter may suggest a contrived quality not consonant with sincerity—the frequent lapses into Latin and Greek, and the piling up of examples from Classical history of men who, like himself, had sinned in

their youth but later became good members of society. But, if one
recalls Udall's education as a Humanist—he was immersed in
Latin at Winchester and Oxford, and had even been a lecturer in
Greek at Oxford—and if one recalls too that the man who wrote
this letter had already written a successful textbook on Terence,
then the question of contrivance seems insignificant. As a matter
of fact, a fellow Humanist, Stephen Gardiner, probably reflects a
common feeling among educated men of the day when he re-
minds a friend in a personal letter that English is good enough for
everyday purposes; but, when he wants to express himself carefully and strongly, he falls back on the much greater resources of
Latin.

And, when we consider further that an appeal to Classical history was an inherent part of Humanist education in rhetoric, then
Udall's appeals to history can be seen to have been natural to any
Humanist no matter how emotionally distressed. Despite the
differences in fashions of expression between that day and this,
and no matter what the offense was, it is hard to see how this
letter is not at least sincere. But, whether or not this letter had any
effect, it is of course impossible to say. Perhaps the intercession of
friends and the regard of his patron were not effected by this letter. The possibility is strong, however, that either this letter or
some other personal plea brought his forgiveness, for it is not until
after this letter that Udall's career as a scholar really begins. Indeed, Udall not only received his back pay as headmaster of Eton,
but Richard Cox even paid two pounds toward Udall's debts
there. And in September, 1542, only a year and six months after
his appearance before the Privy Council, Udall's career begins in
earnest with his name being prominently displayed on the title
page of his *Apophthegmes.*

III   *After the Trial*

How long Udall remained in the Marshalsea it is impossible to
say in the absence of surviving records, but he may well have
made a trip to the north of England after his release. Both John
Udall and Robert Aldridge, possible patrons, were in the north at
the time. In addition, an undated poem by John Leland refers to
Udall as being in the north during a warlike period.[11]

Leland's poem reads, in translation [the italics are mine]:

"Udall, companion of the Nine Muses, who loves with his whole being the learned writings, I may in truth call the stars evil now, because they have, together with ill-intentioned fate, taken away from me so true a friend; one who was *a friend so long and so close,* transferred to the inflexible *Brigantes,* where, I think, the Muses hardly ever visit. *For Mars rules there, and plies a bloody sword, wounding with his strong arm Scots and Britons.* What do Muses have to do with furious Mars? But if fate is against your returning to your sweet home, I pray that under your patronage the barbarous North may flourish with your learning, which is valuable anywhere." [12]

The words of the poem of especial significance are "a friend so long and so close," a friendship almost twenty years old in 1541, "Brigantes," and "For Mars rules there, and plies a bloody sword, wounding with his strong arm Scots and Britons." Clearly, Leland addresses an old friend who had gone north where war was underway on the Scottish border. "Brigantes" were, according to Tacitus, the most northern and powerful people in Roman Britain, and not only would Leland have been familiar with Tacitus, but he had once proposed a book on the identification of British place names in classical authors. And during 1541 and 1542 there were active hostilities on the Scottish border, culminating in the Battle of Solway Mass, November 24, 1542.

Altogether, then, a flight to a patron, or a friend, in the north of England, and then a period of intense work culling selections from Erasmus' *Apophthegetema* seem to be the most reasonable guesses as to what Udall was doing between his release from the Marshalsea and the appearance of *Apophthegmes* in September of 1542.

CHAPTER 6

The Scholar-Translator

I *Relations with Printers*

UDALL'S *Apophthegmes* (pronounced ap′-ə-thém) was published a year-and-half after his dismissal from Eton, and
shows him turning to a new career, that of the scholar-translator.
The book is a translation of selections from an anthology by Erasmus of spoken, as distinguished from written, witticisms or moral-
izations. Years before he had shown great promise as a scholar-
translator with *Floures for Latine Spekynge;* a second edition had
been published in 1538 while he was at Eton and the book's reception had probably encouraged him to pick up again that typical Humanist's activity. And in addition to his personal reasons for
reform and accomplishment, it happens also that the 1540's and
1550's were especially favorable for the work of a scholar-
translator. The Act of 1534 had virtually eliminated the competi-
tion of foreign presses,[1] and the propagandist activities of the
government made translating not only a patriotic duty, as the
translators so often piously describe it in their prefaces, but also a
profession which an able scholar could practice with a good
chance of reaping both honor and profit.

Although the *Apophthegmes* will receive a closer look in a later
chapter, it is interesting to see how it reflects Udall's closeness to
London printers at this point in his career. Even a cursory glance
through the pages of *Apophthegmes* shows how closely Udall
worked with the printer. At least three sizes of type appear on all
but a few pages—a large size for the apophthegme, a middle type
for the comment by Erasmus, and a small type for Udall's notes.
Sometimes a Greek word or phrase is interjected, and Udall's
notes are sometimes run from the margins into the middle of the
page in order to make sure that the reader can follow the references to the text. Printing of copy as complicated as this undoubtedly received the personal supervision of the author, especially

with a printer as concerned with scholarly accuracy as was Richard Grafton. Udall, in other words, not only wrote his book, but followed it closely through the press to be sure that it was printed correctly.

Not that Udall was in any way an innovator in his chosen profession of translating and of seeing through the press works of merit. The connection between the scholar and printer in England, of course, goes back to Caxton. But in the less popular fields of translation—religious books and the classics of Greece and Rome—the English Humanists had a historic example of this connection between the scholar and the printer in Erasmus himself.[2]

Erasmus lived with one of the Aldine printers while his *Adagiorium Chiliades* was being printed in 1508. He became general editor and literary advisor for Johann Froben in Basel in November, 1521. In the will Erasmus made in June 22, 1527, he took particular pains to arrange for the employment of skilled correctors of the press for his works. Further, Thomas Lupset, under whom, it will be remembered, Udall studied at Oxford, saw the second edition of More's *Utopia* through the press. John Foxe, of *Book of Martyrs* fame, and John Bale, the noted propagandist, both worked for a time in the printing shop of Oporinus in Basel. Every student is familiar, of course, with the work with printers of such translators of the Bible as William Tyndal and Miles Coverdale. Other translators, whose prefaces, or the imprints of whose books, show that they were at home in the shops of printers are, to mention only a few, Richard Taverner, William Baldwin, William Copland, and Robert Crowley. I recite these well-known facts in order to emphasize that Udall's activities during the most fruitful part of his career—beginning with the *Apophthegmes*—were in the tradition of English Humanism, and to show that a successful scholar in his day had to have, in addition to the qualifications of a scholar in the usual sense, a familiarity with the actual process by which a manuscript was turned into a book. In short, a good scholar and Humanist in those days had to be a good editor—a good "corrector of the press"—if he expected his work to be published and to reach the public.

Udall undoubtedly knew personally the printers of his books: Thomas Berthelet, Edward Whitchurch, Robert Staughton, Thomas Gemini, and, most intimately, Richard Grafton. Not only

did he spend considerable time in Grafton's shop with the *Apophthegmes,* but both he and Grafton lived in the precincts of the
Grey Friars for at least two years (May, 1547, to May, 1549) as
next-door-neighbors.[3] Grafton was not only a leading printer of
the time, but also a man of scholarly interests. In 1537, five years
before Udall appeared in his shop as a corrector of the press for
his *Apophthegmes,* Grafton wrote Archbishop Cranmer a letter
in which he complained of "deuchmen" who go about printing,
who can neither speak English nor write it; "yet they will be
both the printers and correctors thereof, because a little covet-
ousness that will not bestow twenty or forty pounds to a learned
man to take pains to have the printing well done." [4] Grafton, incidentally, published Thomas Wilson's books, in one of which appears the earliest reference to *Roister Doister*—the famous ambiguity letter that will be discussed later. Among other literary
people who frequented Grafton's shop, Udall may have met there
Grafton's son-in-law, Richard Tottell, of *Tottell's Miscellany* fame.
At the height of Udall's career, as will be seen later, a printer,
Henry Sutton, signed as one of the sureties for his appointment
to a valuable living.

II *Miscellaneous Service for the Reformation*

In 1543, the year after publication of *Apophthegmes,* Udall was
appointed to head a group of scholars, under the patronage of
Queen Catherine Parr, in the task of translating *The Paraphrase
of Erasmus upon the New Testament.* He is sometimes credited
only with translating the paraphrase of Luke and with placing the
Great Bible text throughout the Gospels and the Acts, but he
seems also to have translated the paraphrases of Matthew and the
Acts.[5] He was busy with this book until its publication in January
1549 and revised it for a second edition in January 1552. The book
will be discussed in detail later, for the blending of piety and
learning in *The Paraphrase of Erasmus* and its wide circulation
account for much of Udall's renown in both his own day and for
generations after.

In a preface to one of the Gospels of *The Paraphrase of Erasmus,* dated 1545, Udall thanked Queen Catherine Parr for her
patronage, and the following year he received from the queen—
along with John Hornyold, Richard Strenghfellow, and Richard

Moryson—the benefice of the church of Hartyng, Sussex.[6] Udall and the others quickly sold this source of income for cash, but these fragmentary accounts probably tell only part of the story of Udall's rewards from the queen for his work with the *Paraphrase*.

In 1545, the year Udall dated his preface to his translation of Luke in *The Paraphrase of Erasmus*, he referred at length to Exechias. It may have been about this time that he wrote his now-lost play *Ezechias*, which was performed in 1564 at Cambridge before Queen Elizabeth.

He seems also to have done other work for the Protestant government during these years. In June, 1548, Stephen Gardiner, a fiery Roman Catholic bishop who later became the right-hand man of Queen Mary, preached a sermon at court in which he in effect defied his Protestant enemies. Udall was asked to report the sermon.[7] Two years later, as we shall see, he was called on to give testimony about it. In the same year, 1548, Udall was praised highly in a book by John Bale, the staunch propagandist for the Protestants. Among the books listed by Bale as written by Udall is *Tragoedia de Papatu*, a translation of a work by Bernard Occhin.[8] The work is lost, if it ever existed, for Bale may have been mistaken, as he has been shown to be in other parts of his book. Another uncertain attribution by Bale is a surviving manuscript containing an "answer" to the people of Cornwall. *The Book of Common Prayer*, a major work of the Protestants, began to appear in its early editions in the spring of 1549. Catholic reaction was strong, especially in Devon and Cornwall. Udall may have been asked to write this "answer" to the people of Cornwall, although students of the manuscript are not sure. Udall's jury trial in Cornwall (mentioned earlier in connection with litigation during his Eton years) suggests that he had been at sometime a resident in that county.[9]

In this same year, 1549, Udall was appointed tutor to Edward Courtenay, a royal prisoner in the Tower of London. He was paid for this twenty marks a year (about fifteen pounds). Courtenay, a great-grandson of Edward IV and a Yorkist claimant to the throne, had been imprisoned in the reign of Henry VIII and was not released from the Tower until Mary's accession in 1553.

III *Some Curious Litigation*

These years of activity as a Protestant Humanist are punctuated with several lawsuits.[10] They often do not tell us much about the man, for they are sometimes either incomplete or ambiguous, but they do serve to emphasize the break in his career brought about by the accession of Queen Mary in July, 1553; for with the death of Edward VI and, therefore, of Protestant hopes, Udall not only lost important financial benefits, but his creditors descended upon him. Earlier, as we have seen, Udall had become involved in lawsuits as an Eton headmaster and in 1544 he became involved in another lawsuit. Records show that on September 16 Udall loaned Edward Clement, a Somersetshire gentleman, fifty pounds. Immediately afterward he had to borrow forty pounds from Thomas Day, a London wax chandler, and shortly thereafter £4.17.0 from Herman Evans, an Oxford bookseller. The debts were to be settled by Christmas, but Clement did not pay; so everyone but Clement suffered. Day and Evans got judgments against Udall in 1548 and 1554, respectively; Udall got a judgment against Clement in 1545 and again in 1550. The outcome of this litigation has not been discovered.

An even stranger lawsuit had its beginnings on June 10, 1546. Udall borrowed ten pounds from William Martyn, gentleman, of London, and for security gave him a ring worth four pounds. According to the peculiar agreement, Udall promised to pay Martyn ten pounds for the ring *"infra decem dies proxime sequentes postquam dictus Nicholaus haberet expendere viginti libras per annum plus quam habuisset die de consecutione dicte bille obligatones per annuitatem, feodum, donum vel aliter quacumque"* [within ten days next after one said Nicholas should have twenty pounds more to spend yearly than he had had on the day of the making of the bond by an annuity, fee, gift, or in any other way whatsoever].[11]

Obviously, when Martyn loaned him the ten pounds he, and Udall too, must have been pretty certain that Udall's fortunes were on the rise. Martyn brought suit in 1554, and claimed that Udall was in fact receiving twenty pounds more a year on June 10, 1553, and should, therefore, have paid Martyn ten pounds for recovery of the ring on June 20, 1553. At that date, Udall was at the height of his fame; and there seems to be, from this distance in time, no reason for Udall not to have paid Martyn what he owed him. In any case, Martyn's 1554 suit continued, Udall did not pay him, and in the Trinity Term following (January, 1554—the first January of Mary's reign) he brought suit against Udall. In the memorandum for the Easter Term, 1554, lawsuit, he pressed Udall for the money, not having received any word that Udall wanted either to settle the debt or to postpone the suit for it. Records do not reveal the outcome of the trial, but later Udall is obviously free.

CHAPTER 7

Further Fruits of Reform

I *Udall as Publisher*

IN 1550 occurred three events of great importance to Udall. First, in July appeared his translation of a work by Peter Martyr, *A Discourse or traictise of Petur* [sic] *Martyr*. Second, in the same month, he was granted a valuable privilege to print that book and others, including the Bible. And the third event was his giving testimony in the trial of Stephen Gardiner.

Udall's translation of Peter Martyr came about as a result of Archbishop Cranmer's policy of inviting leading Continental Protestants to England to help with the English Reformation. Cranmer saw that they were given comfortable livings and platforms of national importance at Oxford and Cambridge. One of the men so invited was Peter Martyr Vermigli (not to be confused with the Peter Martyr, no kin, who was an early writer on the discovery of America). Martyr was made Regius Professor of Divinity at Oxford. His lectures and disputations with Romish opponents were published in Latin for a learned audience, and one of his disputations was turned over to Udall to translate into English.[1]

The second event of importance to Udall this year is striking evidence of how completely he had reformed after his disgrace at Eton. The same Privy Council that in 1541 had sent him to the Marshalsea granted him special permission to print not only the work of Peter Martyr he had just translated, but also "the byble in Englysshe aswell [sic] in the large volume for the vses of the Churches within this our Realme and other dominynions, as also in any other convenyent volume." [2] Although it is hard to measure exactly in modern terms the monetary value of this privilege, it was unmistakably an acknowledgement of Udall's status in the world of Protestant reform and Humanistic endeavor. Publishing the Bible in those days, as it is today, was an important publication venture; printers sometimes made fortunes publishing the

Bible (Edward Whitchurch is an example), and it is tempting to speculate how greatly Udall might have profited if he had taken advantage of the privilege, especially as he had permission to print the Bible "in any other convenyent volume"; the popular Geneva Bible owed its circulation in part to its being printed in a convenient volume.

The practical intent of the privilege and an indication, perhaps, of the seriousness of the Privy Council, may be seen in the clause which prohibits other printers "from taking away, under colour of any commission or authority, any compositor or pressman, of the said Nicholas so long as they are disposed to serve him." [3] This clause may have been inserted especially to protect Udall from the kind of privileges extended to Edward Whitchurch and Richard Grafton, who were authorized in 1547 "to take up as manye prynters, composytours and founders as well householders as prentyces and journymen as others they needed for the king's works in their offices." [4] However, with one puzzling exception, Udall does not seem to have taken advantage of this royal permission to print books. That exception is his translation of Peter Martyr.

This book has occasioned special study by bibliographers because of the peculiar status of Udall as the publisher. What exactly was a publisher in those days, and can Udall be called, in fact, the publisher of the book in the same way as the printers of the period can be called publishers? The intricacies of the debate hinge on the meaning of the imprints in books published at the time. According to the colophon, the book was "imprinted at London by Robert Stoughton dwellinge within Ludgate at the signe of the Bysshoppes Mitre for Nycolas Udall. *Cum priviligis ad imprimendum solum.*" Professor M. A. Shaaber, in discussing the book in his "The Meaning of the Imprint in Early Printed Books," [5] points out that it is difficult to unravel the meaning of this imprint since Udall's address is not included. Further, Professor Shaaber also notes that type experts ascribe the type, not to Stoughton, but to the press of Edward Whitchurch.

Summing up all the arguments about Udall's status, the best guess seems to be that Udall was the publisher of this book only in the sense that any author was considered a publisher who made his own arrangements with the printer and bookseller for the composition and sale of his books. Although his close acquaintance with the printers may have made it easier for him to arrange the details of the printing, it is probable that the privelege given him by letters patent was not called into use except for whatever prestige it may have carried. If that is true, his name was included in the imprint as a professional translator and not as a publisher. Whether or not the book was backed with government funds is impossible to say, but since it was printed at the peak of the controversy over the sacrament of the Eucharist, it probably was a good venture from a business point of view.

II *The Charge of Apostasy*

The third important event of 1550—the trial of Stephen Gardiner—has frequently figured in charges of Udall's having been a weak Protestant who turned to Roman Catholicism with the accession of Mary in 1553.[6] Gardiner was brought to trial in December for preaching the sermon that Udall had reported on two years before. A record of the trial shows that Udall's testimony was among the shortest and least harmful of all the depositions of the Crown's witnesses.[7] To the article that Gardiner had been "complained upon for his opposition to church reform measures," Udall deposed "that he had heard say, that the bishop of Winchester was complained upon to the council." As to the article that Gardiner had been enjoined and commanded to conform, Udall replied that he could not depose. And to the articles charging Gardiner with not preaching on prescribed topics, and with preaching on prohibited matters, Udall deposed simply that he had reported the sermon as he had heard it. His testimony has been called lukewarm, but it seems fairer from this distance to see it as only neutral; the fact he was chosen to report the sermon in the first place suggests that he was acceptable to both sides in the dispute. He was, however, a Crown witness, but it does not follow that he was an apostate because he was not pursued to the flames after Gardiner came to power.

Several of the politicians involved in Gardiner's imprisonment and trial, among them Sir William Cecil, Sir William Paget, and Sir Thomas Chaloner, even found employment in Mary's government without being condemned afterward as "timeservers." Two of the Crown witnesses, Sir John Cheke and Edward Hawforde, received honorable positions in Elizabeth's reign, even though when Mary was queen they made a public recantation or subscribed to Roman Catholic articles. There is no record of Udall having done either. Clearly, the fact that Udall was not persecuted during Mary's reign because of his modest share in Gardiner's trial can hardly have made him a turncoat in the eyes of his contemporaries.

In fact, he was praised in print by two Protestant exiles. John Bale not only praised Udall before the trial, in 1548, but he published a book long afterward, in 1557, in which he lauded Udall as a translator who served "the Christian republic" by his writing and translating.[8] Another Protestant exile, Lawrence Humphrey, praised Udall in these terms in 1559: ". . . in collecting the flowers of Terence and translating them elegantly into the vernacular, and in translating Erasmus' *Apophthegmes* and in other works his work was not unfruitful to them, and brought glory on himself." [9] Moreover his Protestant play *Ezechias* would hardly have been resurrected after his death if his name had been held in contempt as an apostate. Finally, he was staunch enough Protestant to have his name carried in Roman Catholic indexes of prohibited books from 1559 to 1900.[10]

III   *Signs of Success*

His activities in support of the English Reformation continued in 1551. During the summer, as he explains in the preface, he worked on a second edition of *The Paraphrase of Erasmus*, chiefly by way of compiling an elaborate concordance. This book was published January, 1552. He was also asked to contribute verses to two books of encomia. The verses themselves add little to his literary stature, being only conventional graceful praises for the people for whom the books were compiled, but his being asked to contribute to them attests to his standing among Reformation scholars.

De obitu doctissimi et sanctissimi theologi doctoris Martini Buceri . . . (London, 1551) is a collection of verses put together by John Cheke in honor of the Protestant theologian Martin Bucer, who had died February 28, 1551, while lecturing as Regius Professor of Divinity at Cambridge.[11] Bucer, like Peter Martyr, had been invited from the Continent by Cranmer to help in solving the problems of the English Reformation. The other book of encomia to which Udall was asked to contribute verses is *Vita et Obitus Duorum Fratrum Soffolciensium, Henrici et Caroli Brandoni*. This book was compiled by Thomas Wilson and other Protestant scholars in memory of the promising sons of a staunch patroness of the Protestant reformation, the widowed Duchess of Suffolk. (The boys had died tragically at Cambridge of the sweating sickness shortly after she had moved there to be near them).

Meanwhile, aside from Udall's writings as a Protestant scholar, the year 1551 is memorable as foreshadowing a growing intimacy with his former student Thomas Wilson that helps to make understandable Wilson's quoting later from *Roister Doister*. The word "roister" is used by Wilson for the first time on record in his first edition of *Rule of Reason*, published January, 1551; and during the summer he helped Udall in a vain effort to obtain a government post for Udall's landlord, John Grenebery.[12] Grenebery gave Udall ten pounds on condition that Udall obtain for him the post of caterer to English troops at Calais. Through Thomas Wilson, Udall got so far as to obtain letters of introduction to the Lord Deputy of Calais, who issued a warrant to the Lord Chancellor to appoint Grenebery as caterer. Udall then agreed to pay back half of the ten pounds if a final appointment were not made before August first. The appointment was not made, and according to the records we have, Udall refused to pay Grenebery the five pounds he owed him. The case was continued until 1553, as we shall see, with interesting sidelights. But this fragmentary law suit is interesting at this point for showing Wilson going to considerable lengths to befriend Udall.

But Udall's legal troubles seem to have done him little harm with the Protestant government, for in December 1551 he was rewarded for his Reformation activities by being appointed a canon of St. George's Chapel at Windsor Castle. It is difficult today to spell out what this appointment meant in terms of income, but it was obviously considerable, and besides it afforded Udall leisure for his scholarly pursuits.[13] Ironically, when the new canon looked over the walls of Windsor Castle he could see, less than a mile away, Eton College, the scene of his disgrace ten years before.

CHAPTER 8

A Protestant Humanist's Final Successes

I *Preaching and Translating*

ALTHOUGH Udall's activities at Windsor in 1552 reach a high point, historically speaking, in the first production of *Roister Doister,* some events earlier in the year have an interest in themselves quite unconnected, at least directly, with the writing of the play. We can be pretty sure, for example, that Udall spent about the first six months of the year engaged not only in the typical Humanist activity of translating and editing, but also in preaching. How we know that to be true has its own piquancy.

In July, 1552, a Royal Commission visited Windsor to investigate complaints that echo curiously Udall's troubles at Eton years before.[1] The dean and canons of the chapter had been selling jewels and vessels. They freely confessed to the charges, but defended themselves by saying that they considered that the chapter property belonged to them. Although several were punished, Udall himself was cleared, for he had been absent during the sales of chapter property. Where he had been during that time is made pretty clear by a royal letter to the chapter in September ordering the chapter to pay what was due him while he had been away preaching. Usually this letter is interpreted as somehow making Udall a special case, but if we remember that chapter injunctions make special allowances for canons who are absent preaching,[2] perhaps the letter was only a royal nudging to impell the chapter to pay Udall what was owed him.

Although this letter is the only record we have of Udall having been a preacher, it is not an unlikely occupation for a Humanist to engage in, especially one who had spent so many years with *The Paraphrase of Erasmus.* In fact, in one of the prefaces Udall writes in strong terms about the low state into which preaching had fallen. A list of preachers licensed in 1548 does not include his name, but he may have been licensed later, or his name may have been accidentally left off.[3]

The wide-ranging interests of a Humanist show in the book he dated from Windsor in July, 1552, for it is not a book about religion or the classics, but instead is an early landmark in medical history. It is usually listed in bibliographies under the name of Thomas Gemini, the publisher and engraver, but, as Gemini himself points out, the text is largely the work of Udall. *Compendiosa totius Anatomiae delineatio* (complete illustrated digest of anatomy) is a manual for surgeons based on scientific drawings which replaced earlier unsatisfactory guidebooks they had had to put up with.[4] Interest in medicine is not an unusual interest among Humanists, and it is not surprising to find Udall doing what he can to advance medical knowledge. And then, less than two months later, this canon of Windsor, who mingled preaching and translating and editing, almost certainly turned to playwriting and produced a play linking Latin and English comedy.

II *Performance of "Roister Doister"*

About the middle of September the young and ill Edward VI arrived with his retinue at Windsor Castle after a fatiguing journey through southern England.[5] Sometime during his stay at Windsor it seems highly likely that Udall put on the first performance of *Roister Doister*. A more detailed "case," as it has come to be called, for that particular time and place will be presented later, but it is pertinent now to introduce a man who may have had much to do with the composition and production of *Roister Doister*. He is John Marbecke, organist and choirmaster of St. George's Chapel, Windsor.[6] He would have been a key figure in the production of *Roister Doister*, for the inclusion in the play of five songs, a mock-requiem, a psalmody, and a peal of bells, suggests that Udall was writing for a group of choristers.

Not only would the master of the choristers have been an important figure in the production of *Roister Doister*, even if he had been a stranger to Udall, but John Marbecke seems to have been on friendly terms with him. In Marbecke's *Book of Notes and Commonplaces*, printed in 1581 long after his death, he quotes extensively from Udall's books.[7] One long interesting quotation, mostly from one of Udall's prefaces in *The Paraphrase of Erasmus*, contains words not found in the original, as though he were using either an edition now lost, or a manuscript version or, for that matter, that he knew it well enough to quote from memory. In any case, he was the kind of man you might expect to be friendly with Udall, for he was a frustrated scholar and an intense Protestant. Although his name is written large in histories of church music, it is a common-place of his biographers that he finally gave up his music to devote all of his time to religious controversy. To sum it all up briefly, we have at this point in Udall's career the time and place and probably a willing and useful ally in putting on the first performance of *Roister Doister*.

III *Inns of Court and Some Uvedales*

Udall's name does not turn up in any connection with court festivities of the Christmas season, but in the following February and March, 1553, we find interesting hints linking his name with the Inns of Court and other Uvedales. Court records show him involved in a suit begun earlier by his landlord. It will be recalled that in 1551 Thomas Wilson had helped Udall in early negotiations for obtaining a government post for Udall's landlord. According to the landlord, Udall had not returned half his fee, as agreed, when negotiations broke down at the last minute. This latest trial was a continuation of the 1551 suit. Udall does not appear in a favorable light, but court records are incomplete and we do not know how the case ended. What is of especial interest in the continuation is that one of Udall's witnesses was a Richard Garth.

Richard Garth was admitted to Lincoln's Inn in 1549 and is mentioned in its records of 1564-65.[8] Since there were Uvedales at Lincoln's Inn at the same time, it is unlikely that Garth did not know them, and probably Udall knew them too. In fact, Uvedales were at the Inns of Court all during Udall's lifetime. The career of one of these Uvedales especially may have had an influence on Udall's career. Thomas Uvedale (whose name is spelled variously "Woodall," "Wodall," "Wodhall," and "Uvedale") was admitted to Lincoln's Inn May 28, 1519. He may be the same Uvedale who is mentioned in 1535 and 1546 as having been appointed to attend court during the French ambassador's visits.[9] A man with the same name was also paid in 1540 and 1545 for his duty as "sewer" at the court on Henry VIII. A "sewer" in medieval times was a person of high rank who served meals at court, although at this period the position may have had little to do with serving meals. This Thomas Uvedale, if he is the same man in these records, was accomplished in French, as Udall showed himself to be in *Apophthegmes*. Moreover, he was high enough in court circles to have helped Udall in his career, and some such kind of court interest appears in the background of many of Udall's appointments.

Revels and entertainments at the Inns of the Court at several periods during the year were customary at the time, and it was not unusual to have plays presented at them. A William Ewedall, or Uvedale (the name is spelled differently in different records) was elected one of the alternates for the office of Master of the Revels in 1547. An Avery Uvedale was elected Butler for Christmas Revels at Middle Temple for every year from 1551 through 1557. It would not be too wild a guess, perhaps, to suggest that Nicholas Udall, either through the Uvedales, or Richart Garth, might have attended some of these entertainments.

IV *Final Months of a Scholar's Career*

But aside from the glimpses afforded by this trial of the Inns of Court and other Uvedales, the early months of 1553 reveal mounting acceptance of Udall as a prominent Protestant scholar. In January Thomas Wilson quoted the ambiguity letter from *Roister Doister* in the third edition of *The Rule of Reason* and included a graceful Latin prefatory verse by Udall in his new *The Arte of Rhetorike*, published in the same month.[10]

> As in Logic, our speech is British,
> So in Rhetoric our words are British.
> Each writer calls the same one father.
> England is their mother and cherishes both.

But the crowning financial reward for Udall's long service in the Protestant Reformation, more generous even than his canonry at Windsor, was his appointment in March as the rector of Calborne, Isle of Wight.[11] In round figures, his new position gave Udall an annual income of between three and four hundred pounds—a far cry, even allowing for the inflation of the period, from the ten pounds a year as an Eton schoolmaster. Interestingly enough, one of the three sureties required in such an appointment (recipients promised to turn over to the government a large portion of the first year's revenues) was Henry Sutton, a printer.

This March appointment to a lucrative living shows Udall at the height of his career. He was forty-eight, a Protestant scholar with books to his credit that were not only educationally useful, but also of great service to the Protestant cause. But this new prosperity did not last long, for in July, Mary Tudor ascended the throne, and the days of Protestant Humanism were over.

CHAPTER 9

During Mary's Reign

UDALL lost heavily at the accession of Queen Mary. Only a year after his appointment to the rectory of Calborne another man was appointed in his place. He was still a canon of Windsor in September 1553, but he had been replaced by the following June. Creditors who had long held off court action as long as he was prosperous descended on him after Mary came to the throne, and he was involved in court suits in the fall of 1553 and the following spring.[1]

Although his career as a scholar was over, records exist showing that he wrote plays for the Christmas season of 1554. One of the plays often suggested as having been written by him during this period is *Res Publica,* a propaganda play showing how good Roman Catholicism is for a country. A skillful case has been made for Udall's authorship, but, unfortunately, the strongest evidence is based on the style of the play.[2] There is no question but that the lines do sound like Udall, and certain aspects of construction resemble his way of doing things, but nothing conclusive can be arrived at with only a resemblance of style to go on; too many misleading ascriptions of authorship have been based on style. Other writers could, in fact, have imitated him. Besides, the fact of authorship would hardly have been kept a secret, yet those who came after him in Elizabeth's reign performed one of his plays, *Ezechias,* before Queen Elizabeth, and that is hardly the action of men who would have known that the same author also wrote a Roman Catholic play.

It is true, however, that between December 13, 1554, and January 6, 1555, that is, during the Christmas season, there were payments made for "certen plaies made by Nicholas vdall," and on December 13, 1554, a warrant of the Queen's directed her Master of Revels to supply Udall with whatever he needed for his plays "since our well beloved Nicholas Udall hath at soondrie seasons convenient heretofore showed, and myndeth hereafter to showe, his diligence in setting foorth of Dialogues and Enterludes before us for our regal disporte and recreation." [3] Since this order is dated at the beginning of the Christmas season and records of payments show entries only from that date to January 6, 1555, i.e. to the end of the Christmas season, it may be that only in that period were plays put on by Udall. However, plays by him may have been put on at court at other times, as the phrase "since . . . Udall hath at soondrie seasons convenient heretofore showed, and myndeth hereafter to showe" suggests. No exact sums appear in the records, but his pay may have been generous: Queen Mary had been a friend of his patroness, Catherine Parr, years before. But there is no evidence that Udall was ever the official leader of court entertainments or that he had a permanent appointment with the court stage.

Aside from whatever payments he may have received for putting on plays at court, the picture that emerges of his income during his last years is not a bright one. On November 12, 1555, he was left forty marks (about thirty pounds) by Stephen Gardiner, and on the following December 16 the once successful scholar was appointed headmaster of St. Peter's Grammar School, annexed to Westminster.[4] Gardiner's bequest, and his describing him in his will as his "schoolmaster," may refer to Udall's freely tutoring Courtenay years before after the government stopped paying him, or Udall may actually have visited Gardiner in his dark days of imprisonment and studied Latin and Greek with him. From the little that is known of the beginnings of what was later to become Westminster School, it appears that at the time of his appointment the school was a struggling institution just getting started. The fact that he was appointed in December, when the usual time for the appointment of headmasters was September, suggests that the school was still in the throes of organization.

Udall lived only a little more than a year after his appointment to Westminster. His name, spelled "Nicholas Yevedale," is listed among the burials of December 23, 1556, in St. Margaret's, Westminster. The same register also lists the burial of a "Katerine Woddall" on December 11. Looking further, other names spelled somewhat like Udall's appear on the register during the years before and after his burial. Once again, as in the scattered records available for documenting the beginnings of Udall's life, the student finds tantalizing connections with people bearing names something like Udall's. Unfortunately, about all that can be said with some degree of certainty about his later days is that he apparently was living in the parish of St. Margaret's during the last year or two of his life.

CHAPTER 10

Floures for Latine Spekynge

Floures for Latine Spekynge probably gives a better understanding of what actually was studied by Tudor schoolboys than the much better known *Schoolmaster*, by Roger Ascham. *Floures* is not a scolding admonition, by a schoolmaster who never taught in grammar schools, of what should be taught; but a good example of what the Tudor schoolboy actually studied. In fact, a perusal of *Floures* explains to some extent that love of words and sometimes exhausting prolixity that are characteristic of Tudor writing. The careful scholarship behind the *Floures* is attested to by the fact that much of the book was used in a famous Latin-English dictionary of 1548: Thomas Cooper's *Bibliotheca Eliotae*. In a preface to this work (which was re-issued in 1552 and 1559) Cooper wrote "To the learned man Udall, by whose scholarly annotations our labors have been lightened in many places, give deserved praise and gratitude." [1]

Floures has been analyzed in detail, and its place in Tudor (and especially Shakespeare's) education has been carefully spelled out by T. W. Baldwin in his *Five-Acte Structure* and *Small Latine & Lesse Greeke*.[2] Suffice it here to point out briefly that Udall designed the book to accompany the study of spoken Latin and the reading of Terence by furnishing examples of locutions from Terence that it would be useful to memorize and understand. Since the most difficult constructions in Latin, as in most languages, are the idioms, it is not surprising that Udall emphasized the importance of translating Terentian idioms by avoiding meaningless literal translations, and, instead, of searching for the equivalent English idioms. Here, as in his later translations, Udall insisted on the necessity of paying close attention to the sense of the author rather than being satisfied with word-for-word translations.

A good understanding of what Udall was trying to do can be seen in the title page and preface. The title page reads:

Floures for Latine Spekynge selected and gathered out of Terence, and the same translated into Englyeshe, together with the exposition and settynge forthe as welle of such latyne wordes, as were thought nedefull to be annoted, as also of dyvers grammatical rules, very profytable & necessarye for the expedite knowledge in the latine tongue: Compiled by Nicholas Udall

Udall describes his intentions in the Preface:

I have added wherever it seemed necessary certain scholia as it were, in which both the sense of the poet is explained and the words themselves not a little more clearly declared. Where any outstanding or elegant metaphor is used, I have indicated it. Where any figure occurs, I have noted it. Where any fable comes along I am not bored to narrate it rather at length. If anything which would especially contribute to Latinity appears, I have not passed it by in silence. If anything pertains to grammar, I have not been ashamed to explain it. If any proverb is interspersed, I have illustrated it. If any formula appears a little different from the common, vulgar, and usual method of speaking Latin, I have given the reason, examples and testimonies being cited wherever the matter demands it, and quoted from the best and most approved authors. Finally, that I may make an end, whatever has been objected that seems to be able to retard boyish ability and judgement in reading, however humble or light it may be, I have sedulously noted it.

The "certain scholia" which Udall added illustrate how concerned he was with giving a lively Latin phrase its lively English counterpart. For example, *Ne ille haud scit quam mihi nunc surdo narret fabulam* Udall discusses in this fashion:

In faith, full little knows he how deaf I am, or how ill I can hear now in this side on which he makes all the clattering unto me. *Surdo narrare fabulam*—to tell a tale to a deaf body—is a proverb to be said of them that labour in vain. And it is the same that we use to speak proverbially, when we hear what we like not, saying thus: I cannot hear in that side; which may be said properly in Latin: *Surdo narras fabulam,* or *Surdo canis.* Verg. (*Floures,* 128^r)

I tu huic quo dignus es Udall translates like this: "Get thee hence to the devil. The words sound thus: Go hence whither thou art worthy to go (as who should say) whither thou has deserved to go. And because they are used and spoken always in indignation, they may be aptly and well Englished as afore, for that is our most used manner of speaking in English. (*Floures*, 128ᵛ)

But aside from the interest in *Floures* because of what it tells us of Tudor education, there is added interest in its foreshadowings of *Roister Doister*. Naturally, one would expect to find some similarities between *Floures* and *Roister Doister*, for they both are drawn largely from Terence, but what is of special interest are those sections of *Floures* that contain ideas which later germinated into important parts of the play. For example, a characteristic of *Roister Doister* is Udall's toning down of Merygreeke's activities to make him resemble more a good-natured English Vice than a self-seeking Latin parasite.

In *Eunuchus*, Gnatho describes a parasite's technique like this:

There is a class of men who set up for being the head in everything and aren't. It's them I track; I don't aim at making *them* laugh at *me*; no, no, I smile on them and stand agape at their intellects. Whatever they say I praise; if again they say the opposite, I praise that too; if one says no, I say no; if one says yes, I say yes. In fact I have given orders to myself to agree with them in everything. That's the trade that pays for the best nowadays.[3]

When Udall was interested simply in a prose translation of this passage for schoolboys in his *Floures for Latine Spekynge*, he translated that passage like this:

Such men do I follow at the tail, and among such persons I do not fashion myself, that they may laugh at me, but, contrary-wise, whatsoever they say or do, I show them a merry countenance of my ownself, and also make a great marvelling at their high wits. Whatsoever they say, I commend it; that if they desire the same again, that also I commend; if a man say nay, I say nay also; if he say yea, I say yea too. And for a conclusion, to be short, I master and rule myself to uphold his yea and nay, and to say as he says, in all manner of things, for that is the next way nowadays to get money enough. (*Floures*, pp. 67ʳ-67ᵛ)

Udall borrows the same passage for *Roister Doister*, but he plays down the parasite's greediness and has Merrygreeke put it this way:

Then must I sooth it, whatever it is,
For what he saith and doeth cannot be amiss;
Hold up his yea and nay, be his nown white son,
Praise and rouse him well, and you have his heart won,
For so well liketh he his own fond fashions
That he taketh pride of false commendations.
But such sport have I with him, as I would not lese [lose]
Though I should be bound to live with bread and cheese.
                                    (Scheurweghs, I, i, 49-55)

Another foreshadowing of *Roister Doister* can be seen in an earnest grammatical discussion in which Udall provides a kind of rough sketch for the character of Christian Custance.

Non auderet hec facere uiduae mulieri, quae in me fecit. *He durst not haue doone unto a wydowe, or a lone womanne, that he hathe done ageynste me.* Vidua, duae is a lone woman and a wydowe, whose husbande is decesed: and bicause women (especially such as haue no husbandes to help & defende them, from iniures and wronges) for the mooste parte be nothynge sette by, but had in contempte, which no man careth for, nor fereth to delude and mocke, therefore he useth here that comparison and example. (*Floures*, 193^r)

Although much of the comedy in *Roister Doister* depends on the stout-heartedness of Christian Custance, yet her appeal to the audience stems principally from the sympathy she evokes as a misused widow. For instance, at one point (IV, iii, 1477-82) Christian shows a moment of panic and calls for her page to run for help against the blustering of Roister Doister. When Tristram Trustie comes in answer to her appeal he finds Christian in tears. After explaining how Ralph Roister Doister has threatened her, Christian says

Have I so many years lived a sober life,
And showed myself honest, maid, widow, and wife,
And now to be abused in such a vile sort;
Ye see how widows live all void of comfort.
                                    (11. 1581-85)

Even more than isolated passages can indicate, the appeal of Christian Custance lies in her situation as a "vidua . . . a lone woman and a wydowe . . . which no man feareth to delude and mocke." Her helplessness as a *vidua* emphasizes the cowardice of Ralph Roister Doister.

Even if we did not know that Udall wrote *Roister Doister*, a close reading of *Floures for Latine Spekynge* would make us suspect strongly that the same man wrote both the book and the play.

CHAPTER 11

Apophthegmes

UDALL'S *Apophthegmes* is a translation of twelve of the oral sayings of the ancients collected by Erasmus in his *Apophthegemeta*. Eight of the twelve names selected are Greek, the other four Roman. Udall adds many notes, and he even differs from Erasmus at times. Another humanist, Richard Taverner, had translated parts of the same book by Erasmus two years before, but Udall's is an independent work. He did, however, make use of a French translation, particularly in showing the value of Classic coins in current terms. His book is a typical Humanist attempt to bring the wisdom and humor of the ancients to a contemporary audience.[1]

In his preface, Udall emphasizes the importance of avoiding a word-for-word translation but, at the same time, of "keeping and following the sense" of Erasmus. He explains that he designed his book especially for "young scholars and students," although he hopes that both the learned and unlearned reader will enjoy and profit from it. In the extracts from the preface that follow, we should note how he expresses the typical Humanist desire that his translation take the place of popular books, referring perhaps to such romances as those of Guy of Warwick, Bevis of Hampton, and Robin Hood. We note, too, that he concludes his preface with a long note that suggests how carefully he and Richard Grafton, the printer, had worked to make the book accurate.

My only will and desire is to further honest knowledge and to call away (the studious youth in especial) from having delight in reading phantastical trifles which contain in manner nothing but the seninarie [seeds] of pernicious sects and seditious doctrine unto a more fruitful sort of spending good hours, and by inviting the same youth unto the imitation of honest exercise to do good if I may . . . If any matter depending of some Greek or Roman chronicle has seemed needful to be expounded, if any poetical fable has come in place, if to any obscure proverb or strange history has been made some pretty allusion needful to be declared—all such things, together with the names of the persons here mentioned, you shall find set forth and added of my own noting. . . .

And to the intent that nothing should lack which to the ease and commodity of the unlearned reader might seem necessary, there is added also a large and plain table in order of the A.B.C. whereby to the name of any person, or to any good matter in the book contained, ready way and recourse may with a wet finger easily be found out. That if any of the premises either the interpreter or else the printer shall be found to have failed, I for my part shall not only think my labours bounteously rewarded, but also acknowledge myself highly bounden to render most hearty thanks if the gentle reader shall of his humanity and honest heart vouchsafe to set his pen and helping hand and to end whatsoever error he shall happen to espy; and in the residue so to accept both our labours as we may thereby be encouraged gladly to sustain further travail in writing and setting forth such authors as may to the reader be both pleasant and profitable.

The ancients included in Udall's *Apophthegmes* are (in the order in which they appear) Socrates, Aristippus, Diogenes the Cynic, Philip of Macedon, Alexander the Great, Antigonus, Augustus Caesar, Julius Caesar, Pompey the Great, Phocion, Cicero, and Demosthenes. Although Udall quotes from many authors in his notes, his favorite is Plutarch. A student of Humanism would find much in his references of special interest as to the reading of a learned man at the time; for our purpose it is enough to point out that Udall was obviously widely read in the Classics, especially those of the Greek writers, and, for that matter, may have chosen especially a preponderance of Greeks as part of his feeling, as a true Humanist, that the Greeks were more worth quoting than the Romans (always excepting, of course, Cicero). We have already quoted from this book Udall's remarks about his once having written as a student a defence of drunkenness, and his complaint that horsekeepers get more reward than school-teachers.

Twice Udall politely disagrees with Erasmus. Once, Erasmus, in referring to some words written in sand, suggests that the saying is not properly an Apophthegmes because it was written, but Udall objects: "Words after such sort and for such purpose written may have the force, strength, and place of words with tongue

Apophthegmes

and voice pronounced (218 ʳ)." In another place he corrects
Erasmus' translation of a Greek word.

When Erasmus mentions Apollodorus, a friend of Socrates,
Udall writes: "This Appollodorus was of Athens a poet that wrote
comedies; there was another Appollodorus of the same city a
teacher of grammar; there were also four more of the same name
but of other countries (22 ʳ)." In several long notes we get tantalizing suggestions of possible biographical import. For example, a
long note on Thersites shows a special interest that would be
likely to be found in the author of the play:

"Thersites was one of the Greeks and came among the more [among
others] out of the country of Aetolia unto the battlefield of Troy: a
great gentleman born, but the worst of feature, of shape, and of favour
that possibly might be, and a very coward. Whom Homerus in his second volume of his work entitled Ilias (that is, of the battle of Troy) described both in words and sense, much like as follows:

> Among all others, to Troy there came
> An evil-favoured guest, called by name
> Thersites, a prattler be you sure,
> Without all fashion, end, or measure.
> Whatsoever came in his foolish brain
> Out it should, were it never so vain.
> In each man's boat would he have an oar,
> But no word to good purpose, less or more.
> And without all manner would he presume
> With kings and princes to cock and fume.
> In feats of arms nought could he do,
> Nor had no more heart than a goose thereunto.
> All the Greeks did him deride and mock
> And had him as their common laughing stock.
> Squint-eyed he was, and looked nine ways;
> Lame of one leg and limping all his days.
> Crump-shouldered and shrunken so ungoodly,
> As though he had but half a body.
> An head he had at which to jest and scoff,
> Copped like a tankard or a sugar loaf.
> With a bush pendant underneath his hat,
> Three hairs on a side like a drowned rat.

And not long after his arrival to Troy, for that he was so busy of his
tongue, so full of chatting and prattling with every king and nobleman

[75]

of the Greeks, Achilles being moved with his sauciness and importunities, up and gave him such a cuff on the ear that he slew him out of hand with a blow of his fist." (180ʳ-180ᵛ)

Another note seems to refer to his disgrace at Eton, although the connection is obviously conjectural:

Neither did Socrates suppose that person worthy to be called a crafty beguiler of men, who of some foolish body (persuaded thereunto) did receive and take either money or some piece of plate which he was not able to repay; but much rather those persons he pronounced worthy to be accounted deceitful robbers of men which by fraud and guile did make each man to take upon them the rule and governance of the whole world; whereas indeed they are but villains and slaves nothing worthy to be had in estimation. This saying much nearer touches Christian princes, officers, and bishops, than the gentles [gentlefolk] of infidels. (6ʳ)

In addition to other notes that reflect the life of the author, there are fascinating references to stage plays and interludes. One allusion, for example, shows clearly that interludes were not put on between courses in a banquet: " 'By Jupiter,' saith he again [Socrates] 'it grieves my stomach nothing at all if I be snapped at and bitten with merry taunts at the stage where interludes are played; no more than if it were at a great dinner or banquet where were many guests.' " Erasmus comments: "This custom and usage even yet still endures among certain of the Germans [(yea and in England also) writes Udall] that in feasts of greater resort, there is brought in for the nonce some jesting fellow that may scoff and jest upon the guests as they sit at the table; with the which jesting to be stirred to anger is accounted a thing much contrary to all courtesy and good manners" (34 ʳ).

CHAPTER 12

The Paraphrase of Erasmus

WHEN Udall began translating the paraphrases of Erasmus in 1543, they had already been printed in seven Latin editions since 1521, and some of them had been translated into German and French.[1] These paraphrases owed their popularity to their being, as Udall described them, "a treasury, and in a manner a full library of all good divinity books." In good Humanist fashion Erasmus had digested and turned into popular form the scholarly annotations of generations of learned commentators on the New Testament. The result was a running commentary, devoid of scholarly apparatus and schoolmen's phrases, by the most famous scholar of the day upon the most important book of the time. Translations of his commentary offered to the vast new audience of the English Bibles that were then being published interesting and enlightening glosses on difficult places in Scripture. Erasmus also offered the new Protestant clergy—woefully inept sometimes, and often possessed of more zeal than learning—a storehouse of materials for sermons. These translations also furnished reformers with propaganda because of Erasmus' none-too veiled criticisms of the Roman church.

A typical paraphrase is Erasmus' commentary on Luke 2:8-14 [I have modernized the Great Bible text, inserted by Udall, and his translation of the commentary by Erasmus]:

And there were in the same region, shepherds watching their flocks by night. And lo! the Angel of the Lord stood hard by them, and the brightness of the Lord shone round about them, and they were sore afraid. And the Angel said unto them: "Be not afraid, for behold! I bring you tidings of great joy that shall come to all people. For unto you is born this day in the city of David a savior, which is Christ the Lord. And take this for a sign: ye shall find the child wrapped in swaddling clothes and laid in a manger." And straightway there was with the Angel a multitude of heavenly soldiers praising God and saying: "Glory to God on high, and peace on the earth and unto men a good will."

The paraphrase of Erasmus, as Englished by Udall, reads:

Hearken now in what sort this humble poorness of birth is altogether full of princely royalty. There was a tower not far from Bethlehem called in the Hebrew tongue the Tower of Ader (as if you should say in English, the Tower of the Flock), and it was so named because, by reason of the good pasture ground that lay in those parts, there was a very great store of sheep and other cattle pastured. And, indeed, of this Tower of Ader the Prophet Micheas also makes mention, as he does of Bethlehem. There were therefore in those quarters divers shepherds that watched abroad in the night season for safeguard of their flocks. Verily even of the thingself giving a good lesson, what bishops ought of their bounden duty to do for the health of the people committed to their spiritual charge, if they will follow the example or steps of Christ the Prince and Head of all shepherds. And in the night time was that same most bright son of righteousness born, which should on every side put away the darkness of the world. And His pleasure was first of all to have his birth known rather to men of low degree, because He was born after a poor sort, and to shepherds, because he himself was a ghostly pastor, rather than to emperors, to kings, to rulers or deputies of countries, to Pharisees, to Scribes, to Bishops. And lo! suddenly the Angel Gabriel stood on high directly over their heads, and beside him also a strange light suddenly flushed and shone round about the shepherds, which was neither the light of the sun, nor of the moon, nor of any candle.

Udall gives a glimpse of his theory of translating when he describes his method of working on the paraphrases. In his Preface to Luke, addressed to Queen Catherine Parr and dated 1545, Udall writes:

And forasmuch as I consider it to be a paraphrase; that is to say, a plain setting forth of the sense of the text with as many words as the circumstances thereof for the better linking of one sentence to another requires, I have not so precisely bound myself to every word and syllable of the letter, but I have taken more respect to the explanation and declaring of the sense, than to the number of the Latin syllables. In translating of the very text I think it requisite to use some scrupulosity (and if the translators were not altogether so precise as they are, but had some more regard to expressing of the sense I think in my judgment they should do better), but in a paraphrase, which of itself is a kind of exposition and commentary, I think it nothing needful to be so precise in the words, so the sense be kept. And this I dare avouch, that if an interpreter should in some place be as brief in the English translation as the author is in the Latin, he should make thereof but a dark piece of work.

The first tome or volume of the Paraphrase of Erasmus upon the New Testament bears on the title page the date January, 1548, but the calendar year date is January, 1549. Normally printers in the sixteenth century dated books according to the calendar year, beginning January 1, rather than the legal year, beginning March 25; but legal, religious, and learned works seem to have been exceptions.[2] *The second tome or volume of the Paraphrase of Erasmus upon the New Testament* appeared in April, 1549. This second volume was chiefly the work of Miles Coverdale (who translated an early edition of the Bible, and whose versions of the Psalms are still part of the *Book of Common Prayer*), John Olde, Leonard Coxe, and Edmund Allen. (Since Erasmus had not paraphrased Revelations, a paraphrase by Leo Jude was translated by Allen "out of the high Douche.")

The first volume, however, was largely Udall's work. It included the Gospels and Acts. He finished translating Luke, the longest paraphrase by Erasmus, in 1545, and translated Matthew and the Acts later. Thomas Key translated Mark, and Princess Mary (later Queen Mary) began translating John, but early turned the task over to her chaplain, Dr. Francis Malet. In Udall's preface to Matthew he defended the paraphrases against such detractors as Stephen Gardiner. "And truly whomsoever I perceive to be an eager adversary to Erasmus' writings, I (as my poor judgement leadeth me) cannot but suppose the same to be an indurate enemy to the Gospel, which Erasmus doth according to the measure and portion of his talent faithfully labour to set forth and promote."

A second edition of *The Paraphrase of Erasmus* bears the date on the title page "January, 1551." Udall, however, after describing how he worked on the new edition during the preceding summer, dates his preface "according to the common reckoning" January, 1552.

Even before the work was completed, the royal injunctions of 1547 directed "that every parson, vicar, curate, chantry-priest, and stipendiary, being under the degree of a bachelor of divinity, shall provide and have of his own, within three months after this visitation, the New Testament both in Latin and English, with the Paraphrase upon the same of Erasmus, and diligently study the same, conferring the one with the other. . . . Also, that they shall provide . . . within one twelve months next after the said visitation, the Paraphrasis [sic] of Erasmus also in English upon the Gospels, and the same set up in some convenient place within the said church that they have care of, whereas their parishioners may most commodiously resort unto the same." [3] This admonition was repeated in the royal injunctions of 1559.

There is abundant evidence to prove that the royal injunctions providing for a *Paraphrase of Erasmus* in every parish were generally complied with. A Dutch traveller in 1551 recorded in his journal that "the regular church service usually consists of a chapter or two from the English Bible and the Paraphrase of Erasmus in English translation." [4] An inventory taken in 1552 of property owned by London churches shows that fifty of the eighty-four parishes whose records are extant reported owning a copy of the *Paraphrases*. Many of the thirty-four not reporting the work may have owned it, but their reports are either illegible or obviously perfunctory. [5]

What happened to the *Paraphrases* in the churches during Mary's Catholic reign we do not know; but, as mentioned above, the royal injunctions of 1559 repeated the 1547 injunctions concerning their purchase and use in every parish. Visitation articles and injunctions throughout Elizabeth's reign continued to insist that the clergy procure for themselves and their parishioners a copy of the *Paraphrase*. [6] In 1569 Archbishop Parker's visitation articles enjoined the procurement of the *Paraphrase*, and his example was followed by visitation authorities in other dioceses in the years 1577, 1581, 1582, 1583, 1584, 1585, 1586, and 1599. [7] In 1610 the Archbishop of Canterbury mentioned in a letter—as a precedent for urging parishes to buy a copy of Bishop Jewel's works—the fact that "in the late queen's time of worthy memory, every parish was driven to buy Erasmus Paraphrase upon the New Testament." [8] There can be little doubt but that, as W. P. M. Kennedy writes in *Parish Life under Queen Elizabeth*, "side by side in the churches lay a copy of the English Bible, of the prayer book, and the Paraphrase of Erasmus." [9] As late as 1843 a copy of the *Paraphrase of Erasmus* was still chained in two churches in England.[10]

The influence of this work on the thought and language of the Elizabethans is incalculable, but it must have been important. It is possible, for instance, that a re-examination of Shakespeare's Bible knowledge will show that much of his familiarity with the Bible may be traced to Udall's *Paraphrase of Erasmus*. In one small emendation I have been able to trace " 'It is as hard to come as for a camel/To thread the postern of a small needle's eye.' " [*Richard II* V, iii, 16-17] to a paraphrase of the Biblical passage in the *Paraphrase of Erasmus*.[11]

The subject-matter of the *Paraphrase of Erasmus* must have been part of many Elizabethans' stock of knowledge concerning the Bible. Just as the knowledge of any widely known book of this period is important for an understanding of the language and ideas of the Elizabethans, so must students of the period take into account this almost forgotten work on which Udall's reputation, both in his lifetime and after, was largely based.

CHAPTER 13

Ezechias

UNTIL a copy of *Ezechias* is discovered, much of what is written about this play must be conjectural. The date of 1545 for its composition is a reasonable conjecture, but only a conjecture.[1] In that year Udall referred pointedly to Ezechias in a preface in *The Paraphrase of Erasmus* addressed to Henry VIII. The king at that time was old and sick (he died in January, 1547) and Protestants were anxious, during the king's last days, that he surround Prince Edward with Protestant counsellors. Ezechias was a favorite Biblical character with Protestants because he could be likened so easily and pointedly to Henry VIII. Like Henry VIII, Ezechias destroyed "idols and images," which the Protestants always referred to as symbols of Romanism. Further, the story of Ezechias afforded Protestants a moral allegory of what happened when a king did not provide for counsellors for his successor. The first son of Ezechias, Mannaseh, undid the work of his father because he was surrounded, according to the Protestants, by wicked counsellors who allowed the people to revert to idolatry. However, when Josias, the brother of Mannaseh, came to the throne, he "by the help of faithful and godly counsellors" applied himself to all goodness and thereby prospered."

When Elizabeth came to the throne the example of Ezechias was again frequently called on by the Protestants. In fact, Sir Nicholas Bacon even referred to Ezechias in his opening speech at the first Elizabethan Parliament.

Accounts of its performance in 1564 at King's College, Cambridge, in the presence of Queen Elizabeth indicate that it was chiefly a piece found appropriate to be performed at that particular time in connection with the controversy then going on between the moderate bishops supported by Queen Elizabeth and the extreme Protestants. The controversy was mainly over the preservation in churches of such signs of Roman Catholicism as what the Extremists called "idols" and "images." A short translation of a Latin account gives the gist of what the play was about.

There was exhibited on this night (August 8, 1564) that heroic deed of Hezekiah, who inflamed with zeal for the divine honor, crushed the brazen image of the serpent. From this sacred fount Nicholas Udall drew as much as he thought fitting for the proper magnitude of comedy, put it entirely into English verse, and gave it the name of *Ezechias*. It was truly amazing how much wit there was in it, how much charm in a subject so solemn and holy and, yet without once breaking off the definite sequence of reality. The Queen deigned to be present. Again, only students of King's College acted. But after the performance had been viewed long enough, it was time for rest." [2]

Obviously, many questions arise about this play which can never be answered until the play itself should happen to be found. Why, for example, is the play called a "comedy?" Why did the audience apparently leave for rest "after the performance had been viewed long enough?"

Since speculation about a lost play is largely fruitless, no matter how interesting and unimpeded by a knowledge of the facts, most of the questions will probably remain unanswered. One question, however, can be given a reasonable answer, because it can be supported with some degree of conviction. Why was Udall's play chosen? Since the general tenor of the accounts makes clear that the play was in agreement with the Queen's moderate, if rather puzzling position, the play was probably chosen to show the general support of her point of view as opposed to the point of view of the radical elements among Protestant leaders.[3] Further, since most King's men came from Eton, it is conceivable that they would look first for such a play among the works of a former eminent headmaster. The significance of *Ezechias* having been put on before Elizabeth may lie, therefore, in the fact that Udall was remembered after his death as both a dramatist and a supporter of the moderate Protestant point of view.

CHAPTER 14

Peter Martyr

UDALL'S *A discourse or traictise of Petur Martyr Vermill concernynge the Sacrament of the Lordes Supper* grew out of a disputation at Oxford in the spring of 1549 on the nature of the presence in the sacrament of the Lord's Supper. Martyr met in a formal disputation with supporters of the Roman faith. The debate, which took place from May 28 to June 1, aroused great interest; and, when Dr. Richard Cox—vice-chancellor of Oxford and president of the disputation—refused to give a decision, both sides claimed the victory. This spread the fame of the disputation even more widely. Martyr published his side of the dispute in the same year in Latin, and it was his book which Udall translated. Although Udall claims in his preface that Martyr had made the mystery of the sacrament clear, the modern reader finds it difficult to follow a controversy which was as familiar in the 1550's as are the debates over the atomic bomb in the 1960's.

Udall recognized the difficulty of his task, even for contemporary readers. He writes: "This book I haue laboured to make as plain as I could do, & therfore in some places I haue either altered or leaft the scoole termes whych otherwise would haue made the thing more derke, & brought it as nere as I could to the familiar phrase of English speakyng, or els haue added suche circumstaunce of other woordes as might declare it & make it plaine" (Preface: * 4 ʳ and 4 ᵛ).

Martyr states the problem succinctly in his first paragraph: How are the body and the blood of the Lord joined with the similitude of bread and wine in the Sacrament of the Eucharist? He then discusses in methodical fashion the four main doctrines advanced at that time as explanations of the mystery of the sacrament. He begins with the doctrine of transubstantiation. This Roman doctrine is based on the scholastic distinction between the *substance*, or imperceptible essential nature of every material object, and its *accidents*, or sensible qualities, such as shape, touch, appearance, taste, and so forth. Transubstantiation implies a mutation of substance but not of accidents, for at the moment of consecration the accidents of the bread and wine remain unaltered, but their substances are changed into those of the body and blood of Christ. Martyr stated the Protestant objections to transubstantiation: How can a body exist in many places at the same time, particularly as the Scripture declares specifically that Christ is enthroned in Heaven?

Martyr then discusses the Lutheran doctrine of consubstantiation. According to this doctrine, the accidents of bread and wine remain unchanged at the act of consecration, but to the substances (the imperceptible essential natures of objects) of the bread and wine are joined those of the body and blood of Christ. Martyr objected to this doctrine on three grounds: it does not explain how two different substances can exist under the accidents of one; it does not solve the problem of ubiquitarianism; and, finally (and this point made consubstantiation more abhorred by non-Lutherans than transubstantiation), if the Lord were really present as this doctrine holds, the sacrament should be especially holy, and not considered an indifferent matter up to the individual to practise or not at his pleasure.

The sacramentarian, or Zwinglian doctrine, repudiated transubstantiation and consubstantiation, and it reduced the sacrament to little more than a perfunctory ceremony in which Christ was not considered to be present in any form. This doctrine was too extreme for Martyr, and his chief objection to it was its absence of a spiritual significance.

The fourth doctrine which Martyr discussed was the one he favoured as best explaining the mystery of the Eucharist. This doctrine, still basic in the Church of England, is that the reception of the bread and wine may be accompanied by a special kind of experience on the part of the soul—but only when the soul is qualified to receive it, and only when the sacrament is administered to an individual who is part of a group. Thus, a sinful person, or one without faith, cannot benefit from the sacrament; neither can a lonely communicant profit from the Eucharist. Christ is present, however, in the sacrament to good Christians; and, just as the mouth receives the bread and wine, so the soul can feed on the body and soul of Christ.

Udall's translation of Martyr's tract was only one of several books published in this period which supported the doctrine of the Eucharist as set forth by Cranmer in *The Book of Common Prayer* of 1549. Others were William Tyndale's *A Briefe Declaration of the Sacraments* and his *The Supper of the Lorde;* the anonymous, but undoubtedly government-sponsored *Order of the Communion;* and Cranmer's own *Defence of the True and Catholike Doctrine of the Sacrament.* The smoke of controversy turned into red flames around Cranmer's body before his doctrine became a part of the Established Church in the reign of Elizabeth. It seems clear, however, that one of the books which helped determine the form of the sacrament of the Lord's Supper as accepted by the Church of England is Udall's translation of Peter Martyr's tract.

CHAPTER 15

A Book for Surgeons

NICHOLAS UDALL made a significant contribution to medical education when he compiled from earlier unsatisfactory books a single manual of great use for surgeons in studying anatomy. Vesalius' *Fabrica* and *Epitome* had been systematic but not practical; Vicary's *Anatomie of Man's Bodie* had been practical in dissection, but not systematic. Udall rearranged them into a fourth that was both systematic and practical: *Compendiosa totius anatomie delineatio*. Thomas Gemini, an engraver by occupation, had published a book with a Latin text with the same title in 1548, but Udall's edition is almost entirely different. Gemini left to Udall and "certain other learned men" the task of compiling, editing, and adapting new texts and of arranging them to go logically with his copies of Vesalius' anatomical engravings.

De Humani Corporis Fabrica (Fabric of the Human Body) by Andreas Vesalius was published in 1543. In the same year Vesalius published his *Epitome,* a slim volume complementary to the first. Both of these books were illustrated with engravings of the human body. The *Fabrica* is often regarded as the book that ushered in modern anatomy, for Vesalius arranged his text and illustrations neither on the scholastic plan—of starting at the head and continuing down to the feet—nor on the principle of describing parts of the body in the order of their corruptibility; instead, he described the body systematically. First he described, with text and illustrations, the scaffold—the bony skeleton; then the muscles, the vascular system, the nervous system, the organs of nutrition and other abdominal viscera, the thoracic viscera, and finally the brain.

Gemini copied the engravings from these two books by Vesalius, and Udall, although he took some of the text by Vesalius, adapted to the engravings chiefly the text of Thomas Vicary's

Anatomie of Man's Bodie. This manual, then used by surgeons, was first published in 1548, although the earliest edition that survives is dated 1577. The book was arranged on the principle that those parts of anatomy were to be dissected first that decomposed earliest: the abdominal viscera, then the thoracic viscera, the brain, and lastly the muscles. This was the "order of anatomy" of earlier writers that had been taught surgeons because of the lack of preservatives at the time. An Act of 1540 uniting the Barbers and Surgeons provided that every year the Company should be provided the bodies of four criminals, and Thomas Vicary was probably the first lecturer to conduct these dissections. Who the "certain other learned men" were whom Gemini mentions in his preface as having helped Udall is no where made evident. Edward Wotton, Padua-trained, and the first president of the College of Surgeons, had been at Oxford with Udall, and there were other Humanists with medical interests at the time who would have been known to Udall.

Although medical historians who have analyzed Udall's work find fault with parts of it—particularly with his lack of success sometimes in fitting Vicary's practical text to the theoretical illustrations of Vesalius, they agree in general that his work was a valuable and significant contribution in medical education.

CHAPTER 16

Roister Doister

ANY discussion of *Roister Doister* necessarily starts with the date, for a watershed in literary history—the ascension of Mary to the throne in July, 1553—separates conjectures about when it was composed. The historical significance of the play, too, needs to be spelled out, for in piecemeal approaches to the play separate characteristics have been in turn emphasized to the disadvantage of others, making of the play a mixture of "influences" rather than the organic oneness of a creative writer. And, finally, the genuinely amusing aspects of the play—lines that still make it playable and funny on the stage—have often been overlooked in the seriousness of analysis.

I *The Date of "Roister Doister"*

The years of controversy over the date of *Roister Doister* have resulted in no "received" opinion. The student sent to such reference works as the *Encyclopedia Brittanica* or the *Dictionary of National Biography* finds them in disagreement; and the many editors of the play differ among themselves. Conjectures range all the way from 1534 to 1554. The latest attempt to date the play reinforces earlier conjectures that it was first performed before Queen Mary during the Christmas revels of 1553-1554.[1] Since this date is frequently suggested, the arguments for it will be briefly noted here; but my own investigations result in the conviction, that the play was performed in September 1552. The play, therefore, was not produced during Mary's reign by a scholar turned dramatist in the twilight of his career, but in the reign of Edward VI by a Humanist at the height of his powers.

The chief external evidence for the date of the play is a quotation from it which appeared in the third edition of Thomas Wilson's *Rule of Reason,* which bears on its title-page the date *Anno*

Domini M.D.L. III. mense Januarij (January, 1553). The quotation is "an example of soche douthful writing, which by reason of poincting [punctuation] maie haue double sense, and contrarie meaning, taken out of an entrelude made by Nicholas Udal."[2] Wilson then gives both versions of the letter from the play: the insulting version that the mischievous Merygreeke read, as if the commas were in the wrong places; and the flattering version that Roister Doister wrote.

The date on the title page of this book, January, 1553, has often been taken to mean January, 1554, because many examples exist from the sixteenth century of the use of the legal year, beginning on March 25, rather than the calendar year, beginning on January 1. Which year, then, did the printer of this book use?

Scholars who take the printer's date to mean 1554 argue that the play may have been written for performance at the first Christmas season in Mary's reign. In support of this view they point to the payments made Udall a year later between December 17, 1554, and January 6, 1555. In addition they quote the warrant in which Mary orders her Master of Revels to provide Udall with what he needs for putting on his plays.[3] Further, they attempt to show that the reference to a queen in the first act of the play is to Queen Mary rather than to Queen Elizabeth: "But when Roister Doister is put to his proof,/To keep the Queen's peace is more for his behoof." (I, i, 69-70). And, finally, they suggest that a reference to a queen in the prayer at the end of the play is to Queen Mary rather than to Queen Elizabeth.

But none of these arguments for a date as late as Christmas, 1553, will stand up under closer scrutiny. In the first place, the date on the title page of the book containing the quotation from *Roister Doister* seems clearly to have been a calendar year date— that is, January, 1553, rather than 1554.

Since both the third edition of *The Rule of Reason,* containing the quotation from *Roister Doister* and the first edition of *The Arte of Rhetorike* bear the same date of January, 1553, and since they were both printed by the same printer, Richard Grafton, it can be assumed that they appeared at the same time. A prefatory verse in *The Arte of Rhetorike* refers to Edward VI as being still alive. He had been dead six months in January, 1554; therefore it seems likely that the verse was written in 1553 before he died.

Further, Wilson's preface to the same book is dedicated to Lord Dudley, who was beheaded on August 22, 1553, but who, in the preface, is spoken of as being alive. It would have been dangerous to dedicate a book to an enemy of the government even if the dedication spoke of him as being dead. Since *The Arte of Rhetorike* can clearly be dated by the calendar year, it seems likely that so too can *The Rule of Reason.* In fact, it is not likely that Richard Grafton printed any books that could be dated January, 1554, for he was in prison in the fall of 1553 and was deprived of his office of Royal Printer in December, 1553.[4]

But these are not the only books printed by Richard Grafton that show his use of the calendar year. Five other books—all of his that can be dated accurately by outside reference—bear dates on the title pages of the calendar year rather than of the legal year. His colophon (a statement at the end of a book giving facts about the time and place of printing) to a *Primer in English* (STC 16047) reads: ". . . imprinted . . . by Richard Grafton, printer to the Princes grace, the .xvi. day of March, the yere of our lord a thousand D. .xlvi." Since Prince Edward became king on January 21, 1547, and since Grafton never referred to him as prince after that date, this colophon must be dated according to the calendar year.

A second book dated according to the calendar year by Grafton is *The Book of the Common Prayer* (STC 16267). This is dated in the colophon March 7, 1549. Special investigations show that these March editions (another printer published a *Book of Common Prayer* at the same time) were printed early in March, 1549.[5] A third book Grafton dated according to the calendar year, as we would today, is *The Order of the Communion* (STC 16456). His colophon reads: "Imprinted at London the eyght daye of Marche, in the second yere of the reigne of . . . Edward VI. By Richard Grafton Prynter to his moste royal Maistie. In the yere of our Lorde M.D. XLVIII." The second year of Edward's reign was from January 21, 1548, to January 20, 1549, therefore, this colophon also carries a calendar date.

A fourth book Grafton dated according to the calendar year is *The Chronicle of Jhon Hardyng* (STC 12767-12768). The title page on both editions is dated January, 1543. A prefatory letter by Grafton, addressed to Thomas, Duke of Norfolk, refers to his fol-

lowing in his father's footsteps in defeating the Scots. Just as his
father had beaten the Scots in Henry VIII's reign,

> Sembleably, by thys your last viage
> Nowe thys last October and November
> Made into Scotland, to their great damage
> It doeth as me semeth, ryght well appere
> That when pleaseth our king to send you thither
> Your house in hys right, is appoynted by God
> To bee to the Scottes, a sharpe scourge and rod.

The *Dictionary of National Biography,* which, from other accounts, seems to be accurate in this particular, tells us that the
Duke of Norfolk "in 1542 was sent to wage war against Scotland
and again wreaked Henry VIII's vengeance by a barbarous raid
upon the border. It was the terror of his name and not his actual
presence, which ended the war by the disastrous rout of Solway
Mass." Obviously, since Grafton's verse refers to the Duke's ex-
ploits of "last October and November" (the battle of Solway Mass
took place on November 24, 1542), *The Chronicle of Jhon Hardyng* was printed in January, 1543—a calendar-year date.

The fifth book which Grafton dated according to the calendar
year is *An Abridgement of the notable works of Polidore Vergile*
(STC 24655). On the title page we read "Imprinted at London . . . by Richard Grafton, Printer to the Princes Grace, the
xxv daie of Ianuarie of the yere of Our Lorde M D L X V I." Since
Edward was "the King's Majesty" and not "the Princes Grace" on
January 25, 1547, which would be the imprint date according to
the legal year, this imprint must be another example of Grafton's
use of the calendar year. This conclusion is supported by the date
of the colophon, which reads "imprinted . . . the . . . .xvi. daie
of Aprill the yere of our Lorde 1546."

We have then five books which Grafton clearly dated by using
the calendar year. But we do not have to depend upon the practice of this one printer alone to suspect that *The Arte of Rhetorike*
and *The Rule of Reason* were dated according to the calendar
year. Not only Grafton, but most of the other sixteenth-century
printers used the calendar year. In fact, a separate study shows
that of the eighty-seven books published in the sixteenth century
that could be dated accurately by biographical, historical, or bib-

liographical clues, all but one—and that a questionable case because of historical nuances—were dated by the printer according
to the calendar year.[6] Historians, including literary ones, are used
to seeing the legal year in government or religious documents;
further, individuals vary in the usage of the calendar and legal
year, but there can be little question that printers as a group
dated their books—except for legal, religious, or especially
learned works—according to the calendar year. Both the 1548 and
1551 editions of *The Paraphrase of Erasmus,* being religious
books, were dated on the title pages with legal year dates; although Udall himself, in his preface to Luke in the 1551 edition
refers to "the common style of reckoning" and dates his preface
January, 1552.

Once the fact is realized that all the evidence seems to show
that *The Rule of Reason,* containing the earliest quotation from
Roister Doister, was printed in January, 1553, by modern or calendar-year dating, then all the evidence which refers to Udall's
activities as a court dramatist under Queen Mary no longer has
bearing on the date of the play. Since a quotation from the play
appeared in a book published before Mary came to the throne,
the conclusion is obvious that it was written before her reign.

We still have the problem of performance, however, and it has
been argued that the references to a queen in the play suggest
that the play was written for performance in Queen Mary's reign.
However, revisions for publication in Queen Elizabeth's reign
would explain these references to a queen. All that would be necessary would be putting in "Queen's peace" for "King's peace" in
"But when Roister Doister is put to his proof/To keep the Queen's
peace is more for his behoof" and substituting "she" for "he" and
"her" for "his" in the prayer at the end of the play. These substitu-
tions could easily have been made without interfering with the
meter. Furthermore, this play is not the only one which, after being written during the reign of Edward VI, was revised for publication in Elizabeth's reign. At least five other Protestant interludes
of the reigns of Henry VIII and Edward VI were "roughly edited," as E. K. Chambers puts it, when they were printed after
Elizabeth came to the throne.[7]

Clearly, then, in view of all these arguments—detailed only because an important turning point in Udall's career is involved—it

seems reasonable to conclude that *Roister Doister* was written and performed before January 1553.

But a period as early as the Christmas season of 1551 does not seem a likely period for *Roister Doister* for several reasons. First, as Professor Baldwin points out, it was the great Jean de Roigny edition of Terence of the following year, 1552, that "would bring Udall in a mass most of the structural analysis upon Terence." [8] Second, one of our chief authorities for the festivities that took place at court during the 1551 Christmas season (and they were especially elaborate and are especially well documented) is Richard Grafton. It is strange that someone so well acquainted with Udall as Grafton would have failed to mention his name if he had written a play for the 1551 court revels. Third, it was not until Udall became a canon of Windsor in December 1551, and, as we have seen, became a resident there in the summer of 1552, that he could have had the support of the choristers and Master of Choristers that seem to have played such a large part in the performance of the song-filled *Roister Doister*.

As was pointed out earlier (Chapter 8) John Marbecke, Master of the Choristers at St. George's Chapel, Windsor, would have been a friendly and useful ally in the first performance of *Roister Doister*. Further, too, it will be remembered, the occasion for such a performance presented itself when the young, ailing Edward VI, fatigued from a long journey, visited Windsor in September, 1552. The lines in the prologue of *Roister Doister:* "For mirth prolongeth life and causeth health; mirth recreates our spirits and voideth pensiveness" may have had especial significance at the first performance of the play. Taking all these circumstances into consideration, and remembering that Wilson quoted from the play in the following January, we have a reasonable time, place, and opportunity for the first presentation of *Roister Doister*—Windsor Castle in September of 1552.

II *Latin Elements in "Roister Doister"*

The historical significance of *Roister Doister* lies, of course, in its being a kind of bridge between Roman and English comedy. The play has often been studied to see how much Udall borrowed from Roman comedy and how much he drew on native sources. It tells the story of a cowardly blockhead, egged on by his friend,

who woos a widow for her money. After a scene in which he and
his servants are worsted in a ridiculous battle with kitchen implements, the widow's fiancé returns from a voyage, and the play
ends happily with everyone becoming friends.

The plot can be traced to the sub-plot of Terence's *Eunuchus*.
In both plays the hero tries to win a woman's favor in her lover's
absence; in both, he relies on the counsel of a mischievous parasite; in both, his actions reach the same height of absurdity in an
unsuccessful attack on a woman's house; in both, there is a general reconciliation at the end. Thraso, in *Eunuchus*, tries to win
the favor of Thais while her lover, Phaedria is away in the country. The parasite, Gnatho, leads Thraso to make such a fool of
himself that he finally attacks Thais' house with an array of servants armed with kitchen implements. He and his comical army are
repulsed by Thais and her servants, and finally Gnatho brings
about a reconciliation. In Udall's play, Roister Doister, encouraged by Mathewe Merygreeke, woos Dame Custance while her
betrothed, Gawyn Goodlucke, is away on a voyage. The climax of
the action occurs, as in *Eunuchus*, in the last scene of the fourth
act when Roister Doister attacks the house of Dame Custance
with his foolish array of house servants. They are put to flight by
Custance and her household; and Mathewe Merygreeke, like
Gnatho, effects a reconciliation between Roister Doister and Custance.

Not only did Udall borrow the plot from Terence; but, as Professor Baldwin has pointed out, he followed the Latin five-act
structure faithfully. In the first two acts, or *protasis,* the main
characters—Ralph Roister Doister, Mathewe Merygreeke, and
Christian Custance—are introduced; and Roister Doister, egged
on by Merygreeke, is seen to be ludicrously determined to have
Custance for his wife. The chief *perturbation* is that Custance is
not only not even slightly interested, but is betrothed to another.
The third and fourth acts, or *epitasis,* show the action developing
in a series of complications: Roister Doister's suit is comically
worsened by Merygreeke's mischievous misreading of his letter to
Custance; and Sim Suresby, a friend of Gawyn Goodlucke, the
fiancé, suspects the faithfulness of Custance because of Roister
Doister's attentions. The action comes to a climax at the end of
the fourth act with the farcical battle between Roister Doister and

Custance. In the fifth act the complications are dissolved in the classical resolution, as Tristram Trustie vouches for the faithfulness of Custance and as Merygreeke confesses that the wooing of Roister Doister was instigated by himself for a joke. Thus is the dramatic structure of *Roister Doister* a close model of the dramatic structure of a Terentian comedy.

Exactly how closely Udall followed his Roman models can be seen by comparing specific passages in *Roister Doister; Eunuchus,* by Terence; and *Miles Gloriosus,* by Plautus. Such a comparison shows at the same time, however, how Udall adapted his sources to an English audience by inserting allusions to heroes of folk-lore and medieval romances, and how he adroitly made his blockhead and parasite more innocently funny than their Roman counterparts.

SANGA: Here, Sir (*comes forward with a sponge*).
THRASO: What, you spiritless wretch, is it with a sponge you think to do battle, bringing one here like that?
SANGA: O Sir, I knew the commandant's valor and the strength of the troops. An affair of bloodshed, says I; how am I to wipe the wounds? says I.
THRASO: Where are the rest?
SANGA: Rest? What the plague? There's only Sannio left at home to keep guard.
THRASO (*to Gnotho*): You draw up these troops; I'll post myself behind the van; from there I shall give the word to all.
GNATHO (*aside*): Now he *is* wise; his arrangement secures his own safety.
THRASO: My tactics are just those of Pyrrhus. (Sargeaunt, pages 315-17)

In *Roister Doister* this passage becomes:

M. MERY: Be not at one with her upon any amends.
R. DOISTER: No, though she make to me never so many friends;
Not if all the world for her would undertake;
No, not God himself neither, shall not her peace make.
On, therefore, march forward! Soft, stay a while yet.

[96]

M. MERY:	On!
R. DOISTER:	Tarry!
M. MERY:	Forth!
R. DOISTER:	Back!
M. MERY:	On!
R. DOISTER:	Soft! Now forward set!
C. CUSTANCE:	What business have we here? Out! alas! alas!
R. DOISTER:	Ha, ha, ha, ha, ha!
	Did'st thou see that, Merygreke, how afraid she was?
	Did'st thou see how she fled a pace out of my sight?
	Ah, good sweet Custance, I pity her by this light.
M. MERY:	That tender heart of yours will mar altogether,—
	Thus will you be turned with a wagging of a feather.
	On, sirs, keep your ray.
R. DOISTER:	On forth while this gear is hot.
	Soft, the arms of Callais, I have one thing forgot!
M. MERY:	What lack we now?
R. DOISTER:	Retire, or else we be all slain!
M. MERY:	Back, for the pash of God! back, sirs, back again!
	What is the great matter?
R. DOISTER:	This hasty forthgoing
	Had almost brought us all to utter undoing;
	It made me forget a thing most necessary.
M. MERY:	Well remembered of a captain, by Saint Mary.
R. DOISTER:	It is a thing must be had.
M. MERY:	Let us have it then.
R. DOISTER:	But I wot not where or how.
M. MERY:	Then wot not I when.
	But what is it?
R. DOISTER:	Of a chief thing I am to seek.
M. MERY:	Tut, so will ye be, when ye have studied a week.
	But tell me what it is?
R. DOISTER:	I lack yet a headpiece.
M. MERY:	The kitchen collocavit, the best hens to grease,
	Run fetch it, Dobinet, and come at once withal,
	And bring with thee my pot-gun, hanging by the wall.
	I have seen your head with it, full many a time,
	Covered as safe as it had been with a shrine;

And I warrant it save your head from any stroke,
Except perchance to be amazed with the smoke;
I warrant your head therewith, except for the
 mist,
As safe as it were fast locked up in a chest.
And lo, here our Dobinet cometh with it now.

D. DOUGHTIE: It will cover me to the shoulders well enow.
M. MERY: Let me see it on.
R. DOISTER: In faith, it doeth metely well.
M. MERY: There can be no fitter thing. Now ye must us tell
 what to do.
R. DOISTER: Now, forth in aray, sirs, and stop no more!
M. MERY: Now, Saint George to borrow, drum dub-adub
 afore!

(Act IV, Sc. 7, lines 1676-1716)

It is evident that, although the plots of *Roister Doister* and
Miles Gloriosus have nothing in common, Udall did borrow from
Plautus for his creation of a braggart soldier.[10] The following com-
parison makes this clear.

PYRGOPOLINICES: Mind ye make my buckler's sheen outshine the
 wonted raidiance of the sun in cloudless sky, that when 'tis needed
 in the fray, the rays may dazzle the array of foes that face me.
 (Act I; ll. 11-13)
ROISTER DOISTER: Sirs, see that my harness, my target, and my
 shield,
 Be made as bright now, as when I was last
 in field,
 As white as I should to war again tomorrow:
 For sick shall I be, but I work some folk sor-
 row.
 Therefore, see that all shine as bright as St.
 George,
 Or as doth a key newly come from the smith's
 forge,
 I would have my sword and harness to shine
 so bright,
 That I might therwith dim mine enemies's
 sight;
 I would have it cast beams so fast, I tell you
 plain,

> As doth the glittering grass after a shower of
> rain.
>
> (Act IV, Sc. 3, ll. 1387-97)

And, in the following borrowing from *Miles Gloriosus*, Udall draws heavily on medieval romances known to his English audience to domesticate his lines. Plautus wrote as follows:

ARTOTOGUS (the parasite): All the women love you sir, and you can't blame them when you are so handsome. Those girls, for instance, that caught me from behind by the cloak only yesterday.

PYRGOPOLINICES: What did they say to you?

ART: They kept asking me about you sir. "Is he Achilles?" says one of them. "No, his brother," says I. "Goodness Gracious! That's why he's such a fine handsome gentleman," says the other one. "Just see what lovely hair he has. My, but the girls could cuddle him are lucky."

PYRO: So they really said that, eh?

ART: Yes indeed sir. The women are a nuisance, with their teasing, soliciting, exsupplicating one to let 'em see you, and sending for me so much that I can't attend to your affairs, sir. (Act I, lines 58-71)

The parallel passage from *Roister Doister* reads:

ROISTER DOISTER:	I am sorry God made me so comely, doubt-less,
	For that maketh me eachwhere so highly fa-voured,
	And all women on me so enamoured.
M. MERY:	"Enamoured," quoth you?—have ye spied out that?
	Ah, sir, marry, now I see you know what is what.
	"Enamoured," ka! marry, sir, say that again,
	But I thought not ye had marked it so plain.
R. DOISTER:	Yes, eachwhere they gaze all upon me and stare.
M. MERY:	Yea Malkyn, I warrant you, as much as they dare,
	An ye will not believe what they say in the street,

When your manship passeth by all such as I
meet,
That sometimes I can scarce find what an-
swer to make.
"Who is this," saith one, "Sir Launcelot du
Lake?"
"Who is this—great Guy of Warwick?" saith
another,
"No," say I, "It is the thirteenth Hercules
brother."
"Who is this—noble Hector of Troy," saith
the third.
"No, but of the same nest," say I, "it is a
bird."
"Who is this—great Goliath, Sampson, or
Golbrand?"
"No," say I, "but it is a brute of the Alie
Land."
"Who is this—great Alexander, or Charle le
Maigne?"
"No, it is the tenth Worthy," say I to them
again.—
I know not if I said well.

R. DOISTER: Yes, for so I am.

(Act I, Sc. 2, lines 206-27)

Finally, in tracing the borrowings that Udall made from Latin
comedy, one of the most significant was his transfer to the English
stage of the sentimental Terentian heroine. It is a commonplace to
contrast the mercantile marriages and prostitute heroines of Classical comedy to the romantic heroines of English comedy, but, as
Professor Marvin T. Herrick has pointed out, it is the sentiment in
Terence that constituted an important innovation in English comedy.[11] Terence's heroines usually turn out to be females in distress
who are rescued from piteous circumstances. Such a character, in
modified form, of course, is Christian Custance, who, too, is a distressed female who is finally rescued from her detractors. In discussing the foreshadowings of *Roister Doister* to be found twenty
years earlier in *Floures for Latine Spekynge,* it was pointed out
that it is the status of Custance as a lone widow—a concept Terence employs—that increases the interest of the play. Her position

sharpens by contrast the farcical actions of a vainglorious blockhead.

III   *English Elements in "Roister Doister"*

The English elements in *Roister Doister* usually receive less attention (especially in anthologies) than the Latin elements; yet
unquestionably much of the effectiveness of the play lies in its
echoes of medieval drama, Chaucer, and popular romance generally. As one critic has pointed out: "When witty page, parasite,
and roisterer came from the Latin comedy to the English drama,
they found figures already known, and popular, which resembled
them, and so they found themselves at home." [12] Tom Titivile, for
example, whom Merygreeke mentions as one of his friends, was a
familiar character in medieval homilies. He appeared also in the
Towneley plays and in the morality *Mankind*. Other common elements in medieval drama reflected in *Roister Doister* are the
boasting of the mummers' plays, the resurrection motif in folk-
drama generally, and the burlesque wooing and kissing scenes.

Udall's admiring references to Chaucer in the Peter Martyr
tract and *The Paraphrase of Erasmus* show that Chaucer's works
were popular at the time even though they presented some lin-
guistic difficulties.[13] A comparison of the Man of Law's Tale with
Roister Doister shows some interesting similarities. For example,
the importance to the plot of the letter episode in Chaucer's story
is mirrored in the plot importance of the letter in *Roister Doister*.
Furthermore, Christian Custance must have reminded Udall's audience of Constance, the heroine of the Man of Law's Tale.

They have similar lines and are strikingly alike in characteriza-
tion. Constance says: ". . . immortal God, thou who didst save
Susanna/Falsely accused" (Man of Law's tale, Part III, Stanza
37); and Christian Custance says: "Thou didst help Susanna
wrongfully accused" (V, iii, 1901). It is obvious, too, that not only
are their names alike, but that Christian Custance, like Chaucer's
heroine, is determinedly constant, and her first name describes the
predominate characteristic of Chaucer's heroine, who is, above
everything else, a Christian.

An attempt has been made recently to see *Roister Doister* as
"perhaps a parody of Chaucer's *Troilus and Criseyda*." With all
due respect to Professor A. W. Plumstead, it seems to me he is on

surer ground in seeing *Roister Doister,* in general terms, as a "satirical parody of medieval chivalric heroes."[14] Certainly, this parody of a medieval knight, on a broad rather than a subtle plane, accounts partly for the humor in *Roister Doister*. It is true, of course, that the play is funny to an audience today, without any background in Roman comedy or medieval romance, but such a line as Roister Doister delivers on his entrance would have been especially funny to an audience of 1552. "Come death when thou wilt," groans Roister Doister, "I am weary of my own life" (I, ii, 1). A couplet at the end of the first chapter in the popular romance Guy of Warwick reads: "But all his time he does to sorrow give;/Wishing each day the last that he may live."

IV   *The Personal Element*

A comparison of *Roister Doister* with its probable sources, then, emphasizes not only the contributions of the Roman classics, but also the essentially English flavor of the play. The Latin elements reflect the interests of a scholar-translator who was not only a special student of Terence, but had spent years translating Latin locutions into their English equivalents. And the English parts of the play reflect the absorption in native literature and drama of any intellectual of Udall's day. (His friend, John Leland, for example, wrote a book defending the historical existence of King Arthur). But in assessing these neatly labelled "elements" it should not be forgotten that fundamentally, in a way typical of any writer, *Roister Doister* is not only a reshaping of other men's ideas, but a creative fusion that is Udall's own. Udall's braggart soldier and parasite are no longer the slightly unlovely characters of the Latin comedies. Thraso and Pyrgopolinices are ridiculous, but their swaggering vanity lacks the saving absurdity of Roister Doister's almost pitiful stupidity. Merygreeke, the "mock-parasite" as he has been called,[15] is less interested in feeding his belly than in having fun with the witless Roister Doister. And despite Udall's stature as a scholar-translator of educational and religious books, his burlesquing of the medieval knight is good-humored, rather than sarcastic or condescending. Finally, the character of Christian Custance, although borrowed in conception, perhaps, from Terence and Chaucer, was made a truly admirable character by a writer who looked up from his "sources" long enough to see around him in English life contemporary counter-parts of the lonely widow in all her defenselessness.

In spelling out these achievements, however, it is not necessary to make more of the play than was probably intended by the author. An innocent play presented by children before a young king for harmless amusement is by its very nature not a piece of subtle comedy. It is obviously unreasonable to mention Udall's name in the same breath with Chaucer, Ben Jonson, or Shakespeare. But, when all is assessed, the fact does remain that here for the first time—not profoundly; not even very smoothly; but, nevertheless, intelligently and amusingly—was a transference from Latin comedy of those forming characteristics in English drama that make *Roister Doister* historically important. Udall's achievement has been summed up by Child in these words: "But when one considers Udall in relation to his sources and evaluates the amount of his indebtedness justly, when we consider what he took and what he did not take, what he did and what he did not choose to do, when we come to realize the measure of his success, we arrive at a much higher estimate of his powers—which, assuredly, considering his historic place, had in them a touch of genius—than if one pays him tribute merely as the author of a play to be considered the first of "regular" English plays." [16]

V *History of the Text*

Roister Doister was apparently not printed until 1566. Thomas Hackett was given a license to print "Rauf Ruyster Duster" according to an entry in the Stationers' Register for the year July, 1566, to July, 1567. Almost certainly the play was printed for Hackett by Henry Denham, or at least Hackett used Denham's type. The play is one of the earliest books printed in a special font used by Denham for years. The puzzling ligature "ée" is a part of Denham's font and can be seen in dozens of books he printed later.

A copy of the play was in the possession of Henry Oxinden of Bareham sometime before 1663, the date he made out a list of his books.[17] Opposite his listing of *Roister Doister* is a note that he loaned the book to Sir Basil (probably Sir Basil Dixwell) on October 18, 1665. Then the play dropped from view until 1818, when the Reverend Thomas Briggs, an old Etonian, bought a copy at public auction and presented it to Eton. There it now remains, the only copy known to be in existence. Briggs did not know the historical significance of the play. The uniqueness of Brigg's find, and the fact that the play represented the earliest regular English comedy were noted by J. P. Collier in 1825.

Curiously enough, the presence of another copy is hinted at in 1922. In the *Nation and Athenaeum*, April 22, 1922, appears this note signed only by the initials "C.K.S.": "Not everyone has the good luck of the owner of a country house who pulled down a modern firegrate, convinced that there was an old-fashioned chimney corner in the background. He found the chimney corner, and in one of the recesses was an immaculate copy of 'Ralph Roister Doister.' It had lain in that recess from the year of its publication in 1567, covered with dust, and only one other copy was known to exist—that at Eton College, which lacks the title page . . ." Years later, in 1940, a plaintive inquirer in *Notes and Queries* asks if anyone knows anything about that "immaculate copy," but so far there has been no answer.[18]

VI *Some Revivals of "Roister Doister"*

Does a modern audience enjoy a presentation of *Roister Doister?* Is this first English comedy still actable? Reviews of American college revivals are difficult to find and assess, but six revivals in England, although reported on in the London *Times* with varying critical reaction, give a clear impression that *Roister Doister* is enjoyable to see on the stage in the twentieth century.

Women students of Avery Hill Training College revived *Roister Doister* at University College, London, on May 27, 1920. The performance was given in illustration of lectures on early Tudor drama by F. S. Boas, the noted English scholar:

It is an amusing and a "live" comedy, the Times reporter wrote. "The first entrance of love-sick Roister Doister, praying death to come; the scene in which the baffled hero "blubs" like a green girl; the heroic scene of the fight . . . all these are still true comedy, witty, hearty, full of the spirit of burlesque and of observation undimmed by classical models. The famous love-letter . . . is still funny, for all its obvious practical purpose as an object-lesson for schoolboys. The many songs help out a very jolly entertainment much more aptly than do the musical 'numbers' in a musical comedy, and the last scene, in which the widow's betrothed sailor-man, newly home from a voyage, has to be cured of his unreasonable suspicion of her fidelity, may be heard in flatter, modern language on half the London stages today. (The *Times*, May 20, 1920; p. 12b)

Another revival took place on January 8, 10, 11, and 12, 1921, in the Abbot's Dining Hall in Dean's Yard, Westminster Abbey. The cast was made up of six members of the Oxford University Dramatic Society, and five young women. Apparently the members of this group were acting in a Pickwickian, or Oxford University Dramatic Society sense. The President of it disassociated the society from the performance, because it was against society rules to play outside Oxford. The *Times* man and F. S. Boas could not seem to agree on the original circumstances of production. "It is stated that *Ralph Roister Doister* has never been acted in public since it was given by the Eton boys before Mary Tudor," wrote the *Times* reporter (Jan. 3; p 8c). Four days later the *Times* gave Professor Boas nearly a full column under a display head for a scholarly discussion in which he pointed out, among other things, that the play had been given only the year before—but probably never by the Eton boys, and only probably before Mary Tudor.

In another review of the same performance given later in the series, the *Times* man began his report of the "interlude with musick and ayres" (apparently quoting the quaint program notes) by referring to the play as "originally acted by the Eton boys before Queen Mary Tudor." He reported that "the comedy is, here and now, still great fun," and praised the costumes as "delightful" and the "singing of the madrigals" as a "thing of real beauty."

A reviewer for *The Athanaeum* was not so enthusiastic about the revival. "*Ralph Roister Doister* (*c.* 1541) is not a masterpiece of humor . . . Apart from the two characters of Ralph and his sycophant, both stolen from the 'Miles Gloriosus' of Plautus, there is nothing alive in it at all, nor does it tell us much about the social habits of the time—except to suggest that the religious revolution of the period entered little into the interests of the common folk . . . Mr. A. L. B. Ashton's setting to the songs, full of the spirit of the period, agreeably tickles the ears. . . . Among the players, who gave an *ensemble* showing scrupulous and skilfull rehearsing . . . Mr. J. C. Ledward stood out head and shoulders as the sycophant, Merrygreek. For easy and delicate comedy it is the best thing perhaps that this accomplished amateur has done."

A "notable" performance of *Roister Doister* was put on at the Lyric Theater on March 31, 1921. Six years later another revival appeared (March 24, 1927), performed by an amateur group; but no criticism was reported in the *Times*. However, a highly unfavorable criticism was written by Gilbert Wakefield, drama critic for the *Saturday Review* of a revival produced by the Malvern Players at the Malvern Festival in the first two weeks of August, 1931.

Ralph Roister Doister is a puerile farce with songs. Its plot is undisciplined, and reminded me of 'Turkey Time' in its reliance on parenthetical buffoonery. Ralph is a vainglorious, cowardly blockhead of the type (derived, they tell me, from Plautus and Terence) which Shakespeare popularized a few years later with, for instance, Andrew Aguecheek; which Mr. Ernest Thesiger's graceful style postdated by a century and depicted as a Restoration fop; and which finds a twentieth-century equivalent in the roles which comedians like Mr. George Clarke play in our contemporary musical comedies. His folly is exploited by a needy humorist named Matthew Merrycheek [*sic*], for whose portraiture (the actor) borrowed from the humorist method of George Robey. Both plays [the other was Hick-Scorner: editor's note] were finely acted and were given an astonishingly lively production . . . and delightful scenery.

On August 1, 1932, the Malvern Players produced *Roister Doister* again. The *Times* correspondent began his combined review of John Haywood's *Play of the Weather* and of *Roister Doister* by writing: "The playwright who dramatizes the English climate is necessarily comical." Later, he wrote about *Roister Doister*, as follows:

Ralph Roister Doister . . . as last year, again represents sixteenth century comedy in the historical series of this festival. Mr. Ralph Richardson repeated his excellent and lively performance of Merry Greek, but he shouted too much and at the same level of tone. Mr. Thesiger's thinner tones are a great help to him in mincing through a "vainglorious cowardly blockhead" wooing. Miss Phyllis Shand, as the nurse, nicely simulated the voice of an old woman, too old, perhaps, but

Tibet Talkapace, though she was true enough to her name, was perhaps too pleasantly soft-toned, and a slight cackle would have made a perter maidservant. Miss Eileen Beldon, as Dame Custance, had a little huskiness that is pleasant to the ear, and she rang a good many changes of expression on it.

This *Roister Doister* tonight was broader than last year's and was definitely farce. Perhaps Mr. Bobby Kerrigan tilted the balance in this direction, for besides the gift he had already shown in . . . the *Play of the Weather* he developed in the comedy the unstable legs that are always one of the stage's best jokes . . . The house was full. (*Times*, August 2; p. 8a)

Perhaps other modern revivals not reported here were better than one suspects some of these performances were, but even behind the sometimes uncritical reviewing one expects of amateur productions the fact is clear that *Roister Doister* is still actable and not without appeal to a modern audience.

CHAPTER 17

Conclusion

LOOKING back over Udall's fifty-two years we can trace the development, even through the fitful light cast by early Tudor records, of one of those Protestant Humanists whose work contributed so much to the strengthening of English thought and literature. Not that his life, anymore than anyone else's, was all of a piece: truth obliges us to record not only his successes as a scholar, but also his failings as a man. Side by side with the achievements of his Eton students we have to record his dismissal from his post for grave misconduct; and as we follow his reformed activities as a scholar-translator we are obliged to note along the way his failures to pay his debts. But close investigation seems to show him not guilty of a heinous crime at Eton, nor of being an apostate of religion: two accusations that have clung to him for centuries.

If he had in truth been guilty of those charges he would scarcely have been able to accomplish what he did, and that was to be a man admired by his former students and respected by his colleagues. What appears to have been almost an accident—dependent on the right combination of circumstances, was the writing of the first English comedy. But from a wider point of view his other achievements need to be remembered.

His *Floures for Latine Spekynge,* pored over by hundreds of Tudor schoolboys, was in itself a Humanist's achievement of no small proportions in the transmission of an admiration for the ancients. His *Apophthegmes,* although less widely circulated than his *Floures* must have had a similar influence. His translation of Peter Martyr's tract on the eucharist was an important contribution in the early stages of the English Reformation; and his editing of a book for surgeons is typically Humanist in its unexpectedness, scholarly efficiency, and educational usefulness. But more

[108]

important than any of these in his own eyes, and probably in the Tudor world generally, must have been his translating of the *Paraphrase of Erasmus*. This work, far more than *Roister Doister*, must have seemed to him and his Tudor readers the single most significant work of his career. Translating, he wrote, is "a more painful and more tedious thing, than for a man to write or prosecute any argument of his own invention. A man hath his own invention ready at his own pleasure without any lets or stops to make such discourse as his argument requires; but a translator must of force in manner at every other word stay and suspend both his cogitation and his pen to look upon his author; so that he might in equal time make thrice so much as he can be able to translate." (*Paraphrase of Erasmus* (1548), a2 ʳ-a2 ᵛ)

Doubtless more than once during the two thousand lines of *Roister Doister* Udall was forced to "stay and suspend both his cogitation and his pen," but a man used to such problems as translating Greek and Latin idioms into English probably did not have to work too slowly. At one place in the *Paraphrase of Erasmus* he writes casually of "philosophers, that is to say, such as know and love God," and "philosophy, that is to say . . . the due knowledge of God." It is significant that he is paraphrasing Plato at the time, for those few words express obliquely what seems to have been the main purpose of Udall's life, as a follower of Erasmus— to make, in the phrase of Professor Bush, "the rational wisdom of antiquity supplement the teaching of Christ." [1]

Notes and References

Preface and Chapter One

1. "Christian humanism [includes] those scholars with a humanist, classical, and rhetorical training who explicitly discussed religious or theological problems in all or some of their writings." Paul Oskar Kristeller, *The Classics and Renaissance Thought*, Martin Classical Lectures Vol. XV (Cambridge, Mass., 1955), 86. See also his "Studies on Renaissance Humanism during the last Twenty Years," *Studies in the Renaissance*, IX (1962), 7-23. I use "Protestant humanism" rather than "Christian humanism" as a term useful in describing Udall's specific career.

2. Udall swore that he was fifteen on January 10, 1520, the date he took the solemn oath all Wykehamists took until 1857. For record of his oath see: H. W. Llewellyn-Smith (ed.), *Winchester College*, publication of Winchester Archaeological Society (Winchester, 1926), p. 8. Three other statements of his age are unreliable. The Winchester entry, from the Register of Scholars, suggests 1504, but the clerk's entries were sometimes copies of other records, and, therefore, may be inaccurate. On his appointment to Oxford June 18, 1520, his age is given as fourteen "in the Christmas season nearest past"—i.e. his birthdate might be 1505, but that too may be inaccurate because of copying at an uncertain date. Years later, in a 1550 trial of Stephen Gardiner, Udall's age is given as "forty-four, or thereabouts." Since his Winchester oath, taken by all Wykehamists up to 1857, was a solemn proceeding, the date he gave then is probably right. Copies of these records may be found in Scheurweghs. (G. Scheurweghs, "Nicholas Udall's Roister Doister," in *Materials for the Study of the Old English Drama*, Vol. XVI New Series: Louvain, 1939).

3. See H. W. Gidden *The Book of Remembrances of Southampton* (Southampton, 1927-1930), I, 77, 79; III, 62; also, A. Wallis Chapman, *The Black Book of Southampton* (Southampton, 1912-1915), III, 54-57; and R. C. Anderson *The Assize of Bread Book, 1477–1517* (Southampton, 1923), pp. 45, 49.

4. Discussion on the connection between Nicholas Udall and the Uvedale county family is based chiefly on Granville L. Gower, "Notices of the Family of Uvedale of Titsey, Surrey, and Wickham, Hants," in *Surrey Archaeological Collections,* Vol. III (1865). Mention of "Nicholas Uvedale" and other Uvedales at Winchester also appear in Robert Lowth, *The Life of William of Wykeham* (Oxford, 1777), and in F. Kirby, *Annals of Winchester College* (London and Winchester, 1892). See also Herbert Chitty, "Nicholas Udall," London *Times Literary Supplement* (July 22, 1939), 437-38. See also G. W. Kitchin *Compotus Rolls of the Obedientaries of St. Swithun's Priory, Winchester* (London and Winchester, 1892), p. 386. I found that *Additional Charter* 40286 in the British Museum refers to a transaction that took place in the first year of the reign of Henry VIII (22 April 1508-21 April 1509) in which Thomas Uvedale of the Soke of Winchester and Henry Uvedale, his son and heir, give security for a loan to a John Brugge, a citizen and alderman of London. The security consists of property at Bromwich in the parish of Titchfield, where the Uvedale family owned property, and a tenement with a cottage in the Soke of Winchester in the parish of St. Peter "called Chessell."

5. "Nicholaus Owdall de Sowthampton in parochia Sancte Crucis xii annorum in festo Natalis Domini preterite." From the *Register of Scholars.* This was drawn up in January from the Election Rolls of the previous August which contained the results of examinations of candidates for election as scholars into the College. See G. Scheurweghs, *Nicholas Udall's Roister Doister* (Louvain, 1939), p xii.

6. *A History of Winchester College* (London, 1899), p. 192.

7. *Vulgaria* was printed again in 1530. Udall probably knew Horman personally, because Horman had been an Eton headmaster and was a senior fellow when Udall became headmaster. Also, John Bale lists "Ad Guilhemum Hormannum Lib. I" among Udall's works in his Scriptorum *Illustrium maioris Brytanniae . . . Catalogus* (Basel, 1557-1559), I, 717. I have modernized the spelling and punctuation of the quotations.

8. "Permittimus tamen quod in festo Innocencium pueri vesperas matutinas et alia divina officia legenda et cantanda dicere et exsequi valeant secundum usum et consuetudinem ecclesie Sarum." (T. F. Kirby *Annals of Winchester College* (Winchester, 1892), p. 503. The translation is from Arthur F. Leach, *The Schools of Medieval England* (London, 1915), p. 153. Details about the Boy Bishop are based on these two books and *History of Winchester College* (London, 1899), p. 182. The quotation about the "dramatic nature" of the ceremony is from Harold N. Hillebrand "The Child Actors," in *University of Illinois*

Studies in Language and Literature, (Urbana, Ill., 1926), XI, 28. See also Arthur F. Leach *Educational Charters and Documents, 598 to 1909* (Cambridge, 1911), xlvi.

Chapter Two

1. References to Udall in Oxford registers may be found in Scheurweghs, and discussion of many of the details presented only briefly here appear in the following books: Thomas Fowler, *History of Corpus Christi College* (Oxford, 1893); Andrew Clark, *A Register of the University of Oxford* (2 vols. Oxford, 1887), and his *The Colleges of Oxford* (London, 1891); Sir H. C. Maxwell Leyte, *History of Oxford* (Oxford, 1892); Charles E. Mallett, *A History of the University of Oxford* (New York, 1924); J. Wells, *Oxford and Its Colleges,* (6th ed.; London, 1904); and, of course, Hastings Rashdall, *The Universities of Europe in the Middle Ages* (2 vols. in 3, Oxford, 1895). Also useful, in a more general way than the title indicates, is John A. Gee, *The Life and Works of Thomas Lupset* (New Haven, Conn., 1928).

2. Terms used at Corpus Christi College are, to a student of Tudor colleges, confusing and exasperating, for at Corpus Christi an undergraduate was called a *disciplus,* although he was called at other colleges a *scholaris.* At Corpus Christi a *scholaris* was a probationary fellow. The special term of *socius* was used to denote a full fellow.

3. Gee, pp. 102-03. Cf. Fowler, pp. 85; 87-9; 370-1; 381, n. 1 Cf. also P.S. Allen and H. M. Allen *Opvs Epistolarum Des. Erasmi Roterdami,* Tom. III, 1517-1519 (Oxford, 1913), 508-09. For the contributions of Vives see Edward J. Baxter, "The Educational Thought of Juan Luis Vives," in *Harvard University Summaries of Theses 1943-45* (Cambridge, Mass., 1947), and Foster Watson, *Vives: On Education,* A Translation of *De Tradendis Disciplinis* (Cambridge, 1913).

4. This John Foxe is not to be confused with the Richard Foxe who founded Corpus Christi College, Oxford. The "lengthy account" appears in *Actes and Monuments,* Fourth Edition . . . Revised and Corrected by Josiah Pratt (London, 1875), V, 421-29, and Appendix VI.

5. See A. R. Moon, "Was Nicholas Udall the Author of *Thersites?*" *Library* s 4 VII (Je. 1926-Mr. 1927), 184-93. See also Frederick S. Boas, *University Drama in the Tudor Age* (Oxford, 1914), pp. 20-1; and A. W. Pollard, *English Miracle Plays, Moralities and Interludes,* (8th Ed.; Oxford, 1927), pp. 213-14.

Chapter Three

1. The play by Sixt Birck does not seem to be like Udall's from the descriptions left us of Udall's, but it is on a favorite Protestant theme—the necessity of kings to listen to godly counsellors. Birck's German play quotes extensively from Luther's Bible translation and is divided woodenly, and not on dramatic principles, into acts and scenes. *Allgemeine Deutsche Biographie* (Leipzig, 1875), II, 656 s.v. "Birck, Sixt," lists six plays by Birck, all published between 1532 and 1539. At least two more should be added: *De Vera Mobilitate,* the dedication to which is dated Feb. 10, 1538; and *Herodes sive Innocentes,* 1538. Cf. A. W. Reed, "Sixt Birck and Henry Medwall *De Vera Mobilitate,* "*Review of English Studies,* II (1926), 412; and Hugo Holstein, *Die Reformation im Spiegelbilde der dramatischen des Sechszehnten Jahrhunderts* (Halle, 1886), p. 126. A special treatment of the origins and scope of this Continental movement is Joseph E. Gillet's "The German Dramatist of the Sixteenth Century and His Bible," *PMLA,* XXXIV (1919), 465-93. See also H. Herford, *Studies in the Literary Relations of England and Germany in the Sixteenth Century* (Cambridge, 1886); The best guide in this field for the neo-Latin drama is Leicester Bradner's "The Latin Drama of the Renaissance (1340-1640)," with its 'List of Original Neo-Latin Plays printed before 1650,' *Studies in the Renaissance,* IV (1957), 31-70.

2. See "Nicholas Udall. English Verses and Ditties at the Coronation Procession of Queen Anne Boleyn," in *Tudor Tracts* (a reprint from Edward Arber's *English Garner,* edited by A. F. Pollard (New York, n. d.), pp. 25-7. Cf. John Nichols, *Progresses of Queen Elizabeth* (London, 1788-1805), I, i-xx. For the probability of Leland and Udall being at Oxford together, see Lucy Toulmin-Smith, *The Itinerary of John Leland* . . . (London, 1907-10), I, viii-ix.

3. For references to other coronations see Robert Withington, *English Pageantry* (Cambridge, Mass., 1918-20), I, 180; 183; *n.* 5 and 6; 190; and Douglas Bush, *Mythology and the Renaissance Tradition in English Poetry* (Minneapolis, 1932), p. 79. The "assertion" referred to is by Edward Arber and quoted by Withington. Incidentally, Richard Cox also contributed verses to the coronation.

4. I am drawing freely here from the account in Philip Sergeant, *Life of Anne Boleyn* (New York, 1924), p. 168.

5. I have put into modern English the verses as they appear in *Tudor Tracts,* pp. 25-7.

Chapter Four

1. T. W. Baldwin discusses *Floures for Latine Spekynge* in detail in his *William Shakspere's Small Latine & Lesse Greeke* (2 vols. Urbana, Ill., 1944). He is not responsible, however, for my surmise that the book had anything to do with Udall's appointment.

2. See Scheurweghs, xlviii. The term "headmaster" did not come into use until long after Udall's tenure; he was regularly referred to as "schoolmaster." In his *Apophthegmes* (1542) he describes schoolmasters as those "that spent their study in humanity," and notes that most men give more wages to their horsekeepers "than to the good bringers up of their children in learning and virtue." (76^r and 51^r)

3. See Sir H. C. Maxwell Lyte, *A History of Eton College* (4th Ed.; London, 1911), p. 580.

4. Recently acquired by the Folger Shakespeare Library, the book bears Udall's signature in his handwriting, and the date "1525," also, presumably, in his handwriting. Miss Dorothy Mason, the reference librarian of the Folger Shakespeare Library, was kind enough to bring this book to my attention.

5. *Ludicra siue Epigrammata Iuuenilia* (London, 1573), 61^r. See also Scheurweghs, xx. The translation is mine.

6. Baldwin, I, 478-79.

7. See Scheurweghs, xxi, who quotes from *Exchequer Accounts,* Receipt Miscellaneous Books, 256 (E/36/256), f 119 v.

8. For the Braintree appointment see Scheurweghs, xxii-xxiii. Aldridge's letter is dated from Eton in October, but without mention of a year. Scheurweghs makes the year 1541; such a date fits in with Udall's dismissal from Eton. However, James Gairdner, editor of *The Calendar of Letters and Papers of Henry VIII* dates the letter 1537. Gairdner is undoubtedly right, for the addressee is Thomas Cromwell, who was living in 1537, but not in 1541. (References to Injunctions, a Garter installation, and a servant by the name of Whalley—all of which fit Cromwell but not Scheurwegh's Sir William Fitzwilliam, identify Cromwell as the addressee.) Further, Aldridge, who wrote the letter from Eton, was indeed there in 1537, but not in 1541, as Scheurweghs' date would have him. See *Calendar of Letters and Papers of Henry VIII*, XII, Pt. 2, No. 848; *State Papers Domestic Henry VIII* (S.P.1), Vol. 125, g. 146-7. Also, Thomas Maynard, *The Crown and the Cross* (New York, 1950), p. 112 (a biography of Cromwell); and A. W. Reed, *Early Tudor Drama* (London, 1926), pp. 25-6.

9. See William Malim's *Consuetudinary,* a description of the customs which were observed at Eton at the beginning of Elizabeth's

reign. It is usually dated about 1560. See Lyte, p. 138; Leach, *Schools of Medieval England,* p. 309; and T. H. Vail Motter, *The School Drama in England* (London, 1929), 50-51. Scheurweghs quotes (p. xxi) the Latin of the manuscript.

10. This quotation is from the 1584 edition, pp. 222-24.

11. See Scheurweghs *in passim* and H. J. Byrom, "Some Lawsuits of Nicholas Udall," *Review of English Studies,* XI (1935), 457-59.

12. See "Outlawry," London *Law Journal,* LXIX (1930), 165-66. Outlawry last appeared in civil proceedings in 1867. The procedure was abolished as obsolete in 1879, but the House of Commons to this day hears a traditional first reading of the Clandestine Outlawries Bill. See also *The City Law* (London, 1658).

Chapter Five

1. The record of this hearing appears in Harris Nicolas, *Proceedings and Ordinances of the Privy Council of England* (London, 1834-37), VII, 152-53; 155; and 157. Since this is a legal record bearing on Udall's reputation I have not modernized it. The "clerk of the check of the guard" was simply the officer of the guard.

2. *Statutes of the Realm,* III, 441; 655; 725; and 749.

3. "Nicholas Udall and Thomas Wilson," *Review of English Studies,* I (1925), 276.

4. See, in the order of the quotations, Lyte, *History of Eton,* p. 111; William Peery, "Udall as Timeserver," *Notes and Queries,* CXCIV (1950), 120; and John H. Blount, *The Reformation of the Church of England* (New York, 1869-82), II, 136.

5. The relationship between Wriothesley and the Cheyneys is based on notices in the *Dictionary of National Biography.* Two additional connections might be mentioned here. Thomas Cromwell married a Cheyney of Buckinghamshire and a Mary Uvedale was residing in 1522 in the precincts of the Blackfriars at the same time as Sir Henry Wyatt, Sir William Parr, father of a patron of Udall, and Sir Thomas Cheyney. Uvedale and Wyatt (perhaps father of the poet) were from Hampshire, and Parr was father to a later patron of Udall. Cromwell's marriage is noted in the *Dictionary of National Biography;* the Mary Uvedale connection is noted in a valuation of lands and goods of the citizens of London in the *Calendar of State Papers*—Henry VIII, Vol. III, Pt. 2, No. 2486, p. 1053.

6. "Rough Copies of the Privy Council Register," *English Historical Review,* XXXVIII (1923), 410-22.

7. A photostat of the register shows this blank where one would expect Gregory's first name or title. Naturally, if a copyist, rather than

Paget himself, made the entry from Paget's notes, the chance of error is even greater. This is a possibility, for although Adair leads one to assume that all the entries at this period were in Paget's handwriting, the "officers of the Public Record Office," at the request of J. R. Dasent, examined the registers and reported that "the bulk" of the entries during Paget's tenure (from September, 1540, to September, 1541) were in his handwriting except "on certain occasions when the services of a professional copyist were employed, as at the beginning of the volume, and in cases where formal decrees of the council had to be transcribed." See J. R. Dasent, *Acts of the Privy Council of England, New Series, 1542–1604* (London, 1890-1907), I, xv.

8. The letter appears in Udall's handwriting in Cotton MS Titus B VIII: 386^r-388^r. The transcription made by Scheurweghs (pp. xxv-xxxii) is here given in my modernization. The letter in Udall's English also appears in H. Ellis, *Original Letters of Eminent Literary Men of the XVIth, XVIIth and XVIIIth Century* (London, 1843), pp. 2-7; W. D. Cooper, *A Supplement to Dodsley's Old Plays,* III (London, 1847), xviii, sq.; E. Flügel, *Neunglisches Lesebuch zur Einführung in das Studium der Denkmäler* (Halle, 1895), pp. 351-54.

9. *The Oxford English Dictionary* quotes this letter for the first examples historically of the use of "lenity" and "fedity." It also illustrates the earliest meaning of "entwite" [rebuke] from Udall's *Apophthegmes* and *Roister Doister*.

10. Wriotheseley had been at Udall's trial; he was a good friend of Stephen Gardiner, who later remembered Udall in his will; and he certainly, as a high public official, was in a position to help Udall. However, not only did he live at Titchfield, but so did members of the Uvedale family, as well as John Udall. In other words, Udall's mention of Titchfield may mean either that he went back to attend a family council, or to visit John Udall. The manor of Bromwich in the parish of Titchfield was held by the Uvedale family since 1428, but in 1530 the Uvedales sold their interest in the reversion to Sir Henry Wyatt. His son, Sir Thomas Wyatt, the famous poet, sold the property to Sir Thomas Wriotheseley in 1538, who owned it at the time of Udall's appearance before the Privy Council. However, court rolls of Titchfield Abbey Manor in the archives of the Hampshire County Record Office at Winchester show mention of Uvedales at Titchfield from 1525 to 1556. The fact that John Udall also lived at Titchfield is mentioned in the *Dictionary of National Biography*. He had been a secretary to Anne Boleyn at the time of her coronation, and he was a close friend of Thomas Cromwell. He was Secretary of the Council of the North from July, 1525, to February, 1550, and he was in the north of

England in 1541. This is the second time that John Udall, whose relationship to Nicholas Udall is difficult to unravel, looms in the background at a critical moment in the scholar's career. Richard Cox not only paid some of Udall's debts at Eton, but he was a tutor to Prince Edward, and later became a bishop. Aldridge had been headmaster just before Udall's appointment. He had been a personal friend of Erasmus and would have been especially interested in the career of a promising scholar. He has already been mentioned in connection with the letter of 1537. He was the Bishop of Carlisle and one of the Commissioners of the North in 1541, and he was certainly there in the north at the time, for letters and money were sent him from London from March through October, 1541 (see *Letters and Papers of Henry VIII*, Vol. XVII, 165-66, No. 258 (f. 50); No. 398; No. 880 (f. 27); p. 351; p. 259).

11. Both A. W. Reed and Ewald Flügel have suggested a northern trip by Udall in 1542, partly because of the intensity of the border wars then. Reed even guesses that Aldridge may have been Udall's patron. See Reed, *Nicholas Udall and Thomas Wilson*, p. 276; and Flügel, *Roister Doister*, p. 92.

12. Leland's poem appears in *Principum Ac illustrium aliquot et eruditorum in Anglia virorum, Encomia, Trophaea, Genethliaca, et Epithalamia* (London, 1589), 33. See also Scheurweghs, pp. xvii-xviii. For Leland's proposal about British place names, see Lucy Toulmin Smith, *The Itinerary of John Leland* (London, 1907-10, I, xxxvii.

Chapter Six

1. See E. Gordon Duff, *A Century of the English Book Trade* (London, 1905), p. xiv. A few exceptions have been noted since Duff wrote, but the generalization is still valid.

2. P. S. Allen, "Erasmus' Relations with his Printers," *Transactions of the Bibliographical Society*, XIII (Oct. 1913-March 1915), 307, 309, and 317. See also Percy Simpson, *Proof-Reading in the Sixteenth, Seventeenth, and Eighteenth Centuries* (London, 1935), p. 31.

3. See Scheurweghs, pp. xxxiv-xxxv. Grafton lived at Grey Friars from about 1542 to his death in 1573. See C. J. Sisson, "Grafton and the London Grey Friars," *Library*, s4 XI (June 1930-March 1931), 121-49.

4. *Letters and Papers Foreign and Domestic. Henry VIII* (1537), XII (Appendix).

5. It is sometimes said that Udall did not translate Matthew and the Acts. See P. S. Allen and H. M. Allen *Opvs Epistolarum Des.*

Erasmi Roterodami, Tom. III (Oxford, 1913), 136-37; and Dr. Helmuth Flexner, *Des Einfluss des. Erasmus auf die Englische Bildungsidee* (Berlin, 1939), p. 87. Udall himself says in his preface to Edward VI (B 4ᵛ): ". . . nothing it is that I do or justly may take unto me as mine act, saving the translation of the paraphrase upon Luke, and the digesting and placing of the text throughout all the Gospels and the Acts (except the Gospel of Mark)." However, in his later preface to the Acts (AAA iiʳ) he writes: "The Actes therefore were no less necessary to be translated than the rest of the paraphrases, which Actes I have by occasion of adding, digesting, and sorting the text with the paraphrase thoroughly perused, and conferring the same with the Latin I have here and there done my good will and diligence to make the English answerable to the Latin book, at leastwise in sense: as by the same occasion I did also with Matthew." Either he corrected poor translations, or hastily provided translations. Apparently he provided translations.

6. Scheurweghs (p. xxxiv) quotes from Additional Charter 8937 in the British Museum, and does not mention Moryson—"a third of the charter has been torn off," notes Scheurweghs. But Moryson is mentioned as sharing the benefice in *Letters and Papers of Henry VIII,* XXI, Pt. 1, No. 649.

7. See James A. Muller, *Letters of Stephen Gardiner* (New York and Cambridge, 1933), 384 and 400. This book and Muller's *Stephen Gardiner and the Tudor Reaction* (New York, 1926) give many details of Gardiner's imprisonment and sermon. For Foxe's account of Gardiner's troubles see *op. cit.* (Chapter 2, note 4), Vol. VI, 24-271. Complementing Udall's testimony on p. 157 are the articles ministered against Gardiner, pp. 64-78; and the "Interrogatories ministered by Winchester against his Witnesses," p. 89.

8. John Bale, *Illustrium Maioris Britaniae Scriptorum* . . . (Ipswich, 1548), 233ᵛ.

9. Scheurweghs (pp. xxxix-xl) is certain the answer purported to be Udall's in MS is not his. Bale, however, lists such an answer, and Udall's jury trial in Cornwall suggests he may have written one. (Bale, *Scriptorum,* I, 717). For Courtenay see Scheurweghs, p. xxxix, and Muller, *Stephen Gardiner and the Tudor Reaction,* p. xxxiii.

10. I have drawn on Scheurweghs and Byrom ("Some Law Suits of Nicholas Udall,") for most of the details about the law suits discussed here. For the Clement-Yerbury suit, see Public Record Office *Lists and Indexes,* Vol. IX (1933), No. LIV, p. 138.

11. Scheurweghs (p. xxxiv) writes: ". . . on June 10, 1546, . . . William Martyn of London gives him a ring of a value of £10, which

was to be paid . . ." and then quotes the section included here, beginning, "infra decem dies . . .". The court record clearly shows, however, that Udall borrowed ten pounds and gave the ring as collateral.

Chapter Seven

1. See C. H. Smyth, *Cranmer and the Reformation under Edward VI* (Cambridge, 1926), pp. 17-25.

2. See Scheurweghs pp. xl-xli; also *Calendar of Patent Rolls 4 Edward VI*, III, 315.

3. This phrase from the warrant is not quoted by Scheurweghs.

4. These writs of aid, addressed to mayors, sheriffs, bailiffs, constables, and other government officers, were issued for one year as part of the government's efforts on behalf of the printing of the Great Bible. Both Whitchurch's and Grafton's writs were dated Dec. 18, 1547. See *Calendar of Patent Rolls 2 Edward VI*, II, 98-9.

5. *Library* s4, XXIV (1944), 120-41.

6. Sir Sidney Lee in the *Dictionary of National Biography* indicts him flatly as one who trimmed his sails on Mary's accession. A recent summing up of the "case against Udall" as William Peery calls it in his "Udall as Timeserver" (*Notes and Queries*, CXCIV (1949), 119-21; 139-41) charges Udall with a kind of career of apostasy, even before Mary's reign. But see my answer, "The Apostasy of Nicholas Udall," *Notes and Queries*, CXCV (1950), 223-36.

7. For accounts of this trial, see Muller and Foxe, referred to in Notes and References, No. 7, Chapter 6.

8. See Bale, *Scriptorum*, 233^r-233^v; and his *Scriptorum Illustrium Maioris Brytannioe . . . Catalogus* (Basel, 1557), I, 717.

9. Scheurweghs (p. xli) quotes Humphrey's *Interpretatio Linguarum* (London, 1559), p. 523. The translation is mine.

10. See my "Nicholas Udall in the Indexes of Prohibited Books," *Journal of English and Germanic Philology*, LV (1956), 247-52.

11. For these encomiastic verses see Scheurweghs pp. xlii-xliii.

12. The *New English Dictionary* cites Wilson's use of "roister" as the first recorded appearance of the word (*The Rule of Reason*, 1551 edition, p. Lvijb). For the Grenebery trial see Byrom, *in passim*.

13. See Scheurweghs, p. xlv.

Chapter Eight

1. See Scheurweghs p. xlv. Also, George F. Townsend, "Some Account of a Visitation of the Royal Chapel of St. George at Windsor, in 1552," *Archaeologia*, XLII (1869), 77-98.

2. Mr. Maurice F. Bond, The Honorary Custodian of the Muniments of Windsor, drew my attention to this point. A copy of the letter ordering the chapter to pay Udall (the original is unknown) is in John Strype, *Ecclesiastical Memorials* (London, 1721), II, 532.

3. A list, corrected and endorsed by William Cecil, of persons licensed to preach during 1548 does not include Udall's name. He may have been licensed later, or his name may have been left off accidentally. Historians have been able to add names to the list. See Richard W. Dixon, *History of the Church of England* (2nd ed.; London, 1881-1897), II (1887), 45-86. See Dixon also [III (1893), 175-6] for the decline of preaching in this period.

4. For a description of this book I have drawn largely on two articles: Sanford V. Larkey, M.D., "The Vesalian Compendium of Geminus and Nicholas Udall's Translation . . ." *Library* s 4 XIII (Je. 1932- Mr. 1933), 367-94; and an introduction by C. D. O'Malley to a facsimile published by Dawson's of Pall Mall in 1959. I discuss the book in more detail in a later chapter.

5. See Hester W. Chapman, *The Last Tudor King: a Study of Edward VI* (London, 1958), p. 257; see also John G. Nichols, *Literary Remains of King Edward the Sixth* (London, 1857), I, 86-7.

6. See Edmund H. Fellowes, *Organists and Masters of the Choristers of St. George's Chapel in Windsor Castle* (Windsor, 1939), pp. 11-21; and R. M. Stevenson, *Patterns of Protestant Church Music* (Durham, N. C., 1953), pp. 24-40.

7. See pp. 163; 763; 791; 828; 964; 1043; and especially 588-89.

8. See H. S. Cartwright, *The Records of the Honorable Society of Lincoln's Inn: The Black Books*, edited by W. P. Bailden (London, 1897-1902), I, 58. For the notice of Garth in 1564-65, see the same volume, page 347. For notices of the Uvedales that follow, see indexes of the work listed above, and Charles H. Hopwood (ed.) *Middle Temple Records* (4 vols. London, 1904-5).

9. See *Letters and Papers of Henry VIII*, Vol. IX, p. 153; and Vol. XXI, Pt. 2, p. 696; Vol. XVI, p. 184, and Vol. XXI, Pt. 2, p. 515.

10. Scheurweghs (pp. 69-72) reprints the letter as it appears in *The Rule of Reason*. He also quotes the Latin verse by Udall as it appeared in the 1553 edition of *The Arte of Rhetorike*, p. 2 r. (The translation in the text is mine.) The Latin follows:

Nicolai Vdalli in Operis Commendationen Tetrastichon
Vt Logice, lingua nos est affata Britanna
Sic modo Rhetorice uerba Britanna sonat.

Vtraque nempe soror, patrem cognoscit eundem
Anglia iam natis mater, utramque fouet.

11. See Scheurweghs, p. xlvii.

Chapter Nine

1. For the loss of Udall's livings see Scheurweghs, p. xlvii; also *Calendar of Patent Rolls, 1 Mary,* p. 3, m. 25; and Henry Chitty, *Registra Stephani Gardiner et Johannis Poynet,* Canterbury and York Series, Vol. XXXVII (Oxford, 1930), 141.

2. See Leicester Bradner, "A Test for Udall's Authorship," *Modern Language Notes,* XLII (1927), 378-80.

3. See Scheurweghs, pp. xlix-xlx; also Albert Feuillerat, *Documents Relating to the Revels at Court in the Time of King Edward VI and Queen Mary. The Losely Manuscripts.* (Louvain, 1914), 159; 160; 166; 289-90.

4. See Scheurweghs, p. xlvii.

Chapter Ten

1. See DeWitt T. Starnes, *Renaissance Dictionaries* (Austin, Texas, 1954), p. 71

2. See T. W. Baldwin's *William Shakespeare's Five Act Structure* (Urbana, Ill., 1947), especially p. 380; but both that book and his *Small Latine, in passim.* I have used his translation of Udall's preface ("Epistle") from *Small Latine,* I, 744-45.

3. See "Eunuchus" in *Terence,* translation by John Sargeaunt, Loeb Classical Library (London, 1921), I, 257-59.

Chapter Eleven

1. This book was published in 1542 and again in 1564. In 1877, R. Roberts, of Boston, Lanchashire, published a reprint: *The Apophthegmes of Erasmus, translated into English by N. Udall. Literally reprinted from the edition of 1564.* See Charles R. Baskervill, "Taverner's *Garden of Wisdom* and the *Apophthegemeta* of Erasmus," *Studies in Philology* XXIX (1932), 155, *n.* 10. Udall quotes the French translation on p. 61^v. See *Les Apophthegmes . . . translatez . . . par . . . Macault* (Paris, 1540), 99^v.

Chapter Twelve

1. See P. S. Allen and H. M. Allen, *Opvs Epistolarum Des. Erasmi Roterodami,* Tom. III (Oxford, 1913), 136-7; also Helmuth Flexner,

Des Einfluss des Erasmus auf die englische Bildungsidee (Berlin, 1939), p. 87. The German translations had appeared in 1523 and 1530; the French version of the *Paraphrase of the Epistles* was published in 1543.

2. See my "The Calendar Year in Sixteenth-Century Printing;" *Journal of English and Germanic Philology* LIX (1960), 439-49. Note also that in his Preface to Matthew addressed to King Edward, Udall refers to "Quene Katerine late wife of your moste noble father, and now of your ryghte dere beloued unkle Syr Thomas Seimour knight, Lorde Seimour of Sudley and high admiral of your Seaes." Catherine married Seymour sometime between the third and seventeenth of March, 1548, and died September 7, 1548; therefore the book could not have come out on January 1548 according to the calendar year.

3. Walter H. Frere *Visitation Articles and Injunctions of the Period of the Reformation* (Vols. II and III edited with the assistance of W. P. M. Kennedy) (London, 1910), III, 10. The 1559 injunctions appear on the same page.

4. W. D. Hobson-Scott, "Josua Maler's Visit to England in 1551," *Modern Language Review*, XLV (1950), 348.

5. H. B. Walters, *London Churches at the Reformation, With an Account of Their Contents*, S.P.C.K. (London and New York, 1939). See pages 77-78; 87; 94; 101; 111; 115; 121; 136; 140; 147; 152; 162; 179; 189; 199; 205; 213; 222; 237; 268; 286; 293; 298; 319; 328; 333; 349; 350; 361; 368; 387; 400; 427; 430; 437; 456; 459; 463; 469; 475; 486; 488; 508; 514; 520; 525; 536; 541; 546; 560; 573; 600; 613; 624.

6. Edward Cardwell, *Documentary Annals of the Reformed Church of England* (Oxford, 1839), I, 320.

7. W. P. M. Kennedy *Elizabethan Episcopal Administration* (London, 1924). II, 57, 111, 125, III, 147, 150, 162, 188, 210, 237, 318.

8. Cardwell, II, 126.

9. (London, 1914), p. 58.

10. "Volumes in Fetters," *Book-Lore*, VI (June-November 1887), 47-8.

Chapter Thirteen

1. The performance of *Ezechias* is described, among other places, in F. S. Boas, *University Drama in the Tudor Age* (Oxford, 1914), and, in more detail, in John Nichols, *The Progresses and Public Processions of Queen Elizabeth* (3 vols. London, 1823). See also Gertrude M. Sibley, "The Lost Plays and Masques: 1500-1642," *Cornell Studies in English*, Vol. XIX (London, 1933). See also A. R. Moon,

"Nicholas Udall's Lost Play 'Ezechias'," *Times Literary Supplement* (1928), p. 289. Scheurweghs (pp. xxxv-xxxviii) includes Latin accounts by Abraham Hartwell and Nicholas Robinson.

2. This account was written by an observer, Nicholas Robinson. The translation, with the exception of one sentence, appears in Sibley (p. 49). The sentence about the play being witty without affecting the piety was translated by myself, after consultation with Latinists, because for some reason it had not been translated by Sibley.

3. For a discussion of the conflicts between Elizabeth and her church advisers, see James B. Mullinger, *The University of Cambridge from the Royal Injunctions of 1535 to the Accession of Charles the First* (Cambridge, 1884), especially p. 188.

Chapter Sixteen

1. The "latest attempt" is William Peery's "The Prayer for the Queen in *Roister Doister*," *University of Texas Studies in English*, XVII (1948), 222-33. Among other suggestions for a date of 1553 or later are Baldwin, *Five-Act Structure*, pp. 380-86; Baldwin and M. Channing Linthicum, "The Date of *Ralph Roister Doister*," *Philological Quarterly*, VI (1927), 379-95; and F. S. Boas, *Five Pre-Shakespearean Comedies* (London, 1934), p. xii. (Boas suggests, without corroborating evidence, that the play was written before 1553, but first performed later "when Udall appears to have been in Gardiner's service.") A date of 1552 is suggested hesitantly by Scheurweghs, pp. lx ff.; and W. W. Greg (ed.) *Roister Doister* (London, 1935), p. vii. Neither Scheurweghs nor Greg consider dating practices in their conjectures. Among those who argue unconvincingly for a period as early as Udall's Eton days are C. G. Child (ed.) *Roister Doister* (Boston, 1912), p. 9; and C. M. Gayley, *Representative English Comedies* (New York, 1930), I, 95-7.

2. Scheurweghs (p. 69) reprints the title page of the third edition of *The Rule of Reason*.

3. See Chapter 9 and Note 3.

4. See John A. Kingdon, *Richard Grafton, Citizen and Grocer* (London, 1901), p. 142.

5. See A. A. Prins, *The Book of the Common Prayer, 1549* (Amsterdam, 1933), pp. II-X. (Pages of this book are numbered in Roman numerals).

6. See my "Calendar Year in Sixteenth-Century Printing," p. 441.

7. *Elizabethan Stage* (Oxford, 1933), III, 177. Chambers lists only four. Presumably the fifth is *Somebody, Avarice, and Minister,* of which only a fragment of two leaves exists. See W. W. Greg, *A Bibli-*

ography of the English Printed Drama . . . (London, 1939): *Nice Wanton*, No. 31; *Impatient Poverty*, No. 30; *Jacob and Esau*, No. 51; *Enough* etc., No. 57; and *Somebody* etc., No. 25.

8. *Five-Act Structure*, p. 398.

9. *Chronicle of England* (1569), p. 1317.

10. See "Miles Gloriosus" in *Plautus*, translated by Paul Nixon, the Loeb Classical Library (London, 1926-38), Vol. V.

11. See *Italian Comedy in the Renaissance* (Urbana, Ill., 1960), *in passim*.

12. See Robert Withington, "The Ancestry of the Vice," *Speculum* VII (1932), 528.

13. See preface to Martyr tract (*4ʳ) and preface to Luke in the *Paraphrase* (A. R. Moon, "Two References to Chaucer Made by Nicholas Udall," *Modern Language Review* XXI (1926), 426-27.

14. "Satirical Parody in *Roister Doister:* a reinterpretation," *Studies in Philology* LX (1963), 141-54.

15. See Harold S. Symmes, *Les Debuts de la Critique Dramatique* (Paris, 1903), p. 3.

16. *Roister Doister*, p. 52.

17. See G. E. Dawson, "Early List of Elizabethan Plays," *Library* s 4 XV (Je. 1934-Mr. 1935), 445-56.

18. See Frank Sullivan, "An Immaculate Copy," *Notes and Queries* (April 13, 1940), p. 263.

Conclusion

1. Douglas Bush, *The Renaissance and English Humanism* (Toronto, 1939), p. 78.

Selected Bibliography

PRIMARY SOURCES

ERASMUS, DESIDERIUS. *Apophthegmes* . . . First Gathered by Erasmus, Now Translated by N. Udall. (1542). (British Museum; Bodleian; University Library, Cambridge; Folger; Huntington.) *The First (second) Tome or Volume of the Paraphrase of Erasmus upon the Newe Testament.* (Chief editor and translator: Nicholas Udall). (1548, 31 Jan. i.e. 1549). (British Museum; Bodleian; British and Foreign Bible Society; University Library, Cambridge; New York Public Library; Folger; University of Pennsylvania; Philadelphia Divinity School).

(A second edition—enlarged by Udall-1551, but dated in his preface, Jan. 1552) (British Museum; Bodleian; Huntington; Harvard; Folger.)

GEMINI, THOMAS. *Compendiosa Totius Anatomie Delineatio.* (Edited and translated by Udall and others). Udall's date in preface: 1552. (British Museum; Bodleian; Boston Athanaeum).

TERENTIUS, PUBLIUS. *Floures for Latine Spekynge.* Selected and Gathered out of Terence and Translated by Nicholas Udall. 1533. (Bodleian; Huntington).

Most large research libraries have one or more copies of later editions that were published in 1538, 1560, 1575, and 1581.

UDALL, NICHOLAS. *Roister Doister.* (Title page is missing). Only surviving copy, probably printed in 1566, is in Eton College Library.

VERMIGLI, PIETRO MARTIRE. ("Peter Martyr") *A Discourse Concerning the Sacrament of the Lordes Supper.* Translated by Nicholas Udall. (1550?). (British Museum; Harmsworth Library; Huntington).

SECONDARY SOURCES

Special articles on Udall are referred to throughout the text, but the following list of biographical and critical writings has been selected as being of special interest to students of Udall.

BALDWIN, T. W. *Shakespeare's Five-Act Structure.* Urbana, Ill.: University of Illinois Press, 1947. This landmark in scholarship contains a useful analysis of the dramatic structure of Latin comedy and what Udall borrowed for *Roister Doister.*

———. *Small Latine & Lesse Greeke.* 2 vols. Urbana, Ill.: University of Illinois Press, 1944. This indispensable discussion of Tudor education contains an analysis of Udall's *Floures for Latine Spekynge.* Highly readable.

BENNETT, H. S. *English Books and Readers.* Cambridge: Cambridge University Press, 1952. An enlightening survey of book publishing and reading in the Tudor period.

BOAS, F. S. *An Introduction to Tudor Drama.* Oxford: Clarendon Press, 1933. An important survey of Tudor drama that emphasizes connections between early and late writings.

———. *University Drama in the Tudor Age.* Oxford: Clarendon Press, 1914. About the only satisfactory treatment of this subject, but a follow-up of the questions raised is still to come.

BRADNER, LEICESTER. "The Latin Drama of the Renaissance (1340-1640)," *Studies in the Renaissance,* IV (1957), 31-54. A useful and well-written synthesis of a thorny subject by an expert in the field. His other writings are also important for students of early Tudor drama.

BUSH, DOUGLAS. *Mythology and the Renaissance Tradition in English Poetry.* Minneapolis, Minn.: University of Minnesota Press, 1932. A brilliant scholar writes entertainingly of some formative influences in literature of especial importance in the time of Udall.

BUSH, DOUGLAS. *The Renaissance and English Humanism.* Toronto: University of Toronto Press, 1939. A clear-sighted definition of both terms. The author manages to re-create some of the Renaissance excitement generated by a resurgence of interest in the classics.

CHAMBERS, E. K. *The Mediaeval Stage.* 2 vols. Oxford: Clarendon Press, 1903. Invaluable brief summaries of most problems of early Tudor drama. Also indispensable is his book listed next.

———. *The Elizabethan Stage.* 4 vols. Oxford: Clarendon Press, 1923.

CHAPMAN, HESTER W. *The Last Tudor King: A study of Edward VI.* London: Jonathan Cape, 1958. An up-to-date, objective account of the life of a pathetic figure, with careful but brief sidelights on the men who surrounded him.

CONLEY, C. H. *The First English Translations of the Classics.* New Haven, Conn.: Yale University Press, 1927. An attempt to spell out the books and atmosphere that surrounded English humanists. Recent studies have revised some conclusions, but this is an admirable account of an important movement.

EDGERTON, WILLIAM L. "The Apostasy of Nicholas Udall," *Notes and Queries,* CXCV (1950), 223-36. Here I attempt to answer charges that Udall changed his religion to fit circumstances.

————. "The Calendar Year in Sixteenth-Century Printing," *Journal of English and Germanic Philology,* LIX (1960), 439-49. This article spells out the extent to which printers used the calendar year in dating their books. It was a necessary preliminary to ascertaining the date of *Roister Doister* because of the date on the title-page of the book in which *Roister Doister* is first quoted.

————. "Nicholas Udall in the Indexes of Prohibited Books," *Journal of English and Germanic Philology,* LV (1956), 247-52. A tracing of Udall's name as it was carried in indexes from the sixteenth to the twentieth century. "Shakespeare and the 'Needle's Eye'," *Modern Language Notes,* LXVI (1951), 549-50. Here I suggest a connection between Shakespeare and *The Paraphrase of Erasmus.*

FARNHAM, WILLIAM. "Medieval Comic Spirit in the English Renaissance," in *Joseph Q. Adams Memorial Studies,* edited by James G. McManaway, Giles E. Dawson, and Edwin H. Willoughby. Washington, D.C.: Folger Shakespeare Library, 1948. A careful and provocative study that corrects many generalizations made for years in literary histories.

FOWLER, THOMAS. *The History of Corpus Christi College.* Oxford: Clarendon Press, 1893. A well-documented book based on materials not readily accessible. Later editions add valuable notes.

GEE, JOHN A. *The Life and Times of Thomas Lupset.* New Haven, Conn.: Yale University Press, 1928. A forgotten figure of humanism is brought to life in a way that shows his significance as a connecting figure between two generations.

GILLET, JOSEPH E. "The German Dramatist of the Sixteenth Century and His Bible," *PMLA* XXIV (1919), 465-93. The earliest, and still among the best studies in English of a subject that needs further attention.

GREG, SIR WALTER. *Roister Doister.* Malone Society edition. London: Oxford University Press, 1935. Based on the Eton copy, this edition gives particular attention to bibliographical problems. It does not, however, retain the ligature *ée* of the original.

HARBAGE, ALFRED. *Shakespeare and the Rival Traditions.* New York: Macmillan, 1952. Udall receives short-shrift in this book, for the emphasis is on popular drama, but it is, like everything Harbage writes, a model for students in its thoroughness and style.

HERFORD, C. H. *Studies in the Literary Relations of England and Germany in the Sixteenth Century.* Cambridge: Cambridge University Press, 1886. This antedates the flood of comparative studies by years, but it is still referred to as if it were written yesterday.

HERRICK, MARVIN T. *Italian Comedy in the Renaissance.* Urbana, Ill.: University of Illinois Press, 1960. One of the best studies available for spelling out the connections between Italian and English drama in the sixteenth century.

LEACH, ARTHUR F. *The Schools of Medieval England.* London: Macmillan, 1915. Important background reading for an understanding of Tudor education.

LYTE, SIR H. C. MAXWELL. *A History of Eton College.* Fourth edition. London: Macmillan, 1911. Not only Eton, but other schools are discussed informedly by a careful student.

MCKERROW, RONALD B. *An Introduction to Bibliography for Literary Students.* Oxford: Clarendon Press, 1927. This classic is "discovered" every year by delighted students. It is a model of how to write clearly and entertainingly about a difficult subject, and is, of course, fundamental to a study of early printing.

MOTTER, T. H. VAIL. *The School Drama in England.* London: Longmans, Green, 1929. A comprehensive survey now somewhat out-of-date, but a necessary complement to later surveys of Tudor drama.

MULLER, JAMES A. *Stephen Gardiner and the Tudor Reaction.* New York: Macmillan, 1926. A scholarly life of a controversial figure who lived in controversial times.

REED, A. W. *Early Tudor Drama.* London: Methuen, 1926. With apparently casual, but carefully exact notes on More and the Rastells, the meaning of "interlude," and early printing practices, Reed makes the reader intensely interested. A reprint is long overdue.

SCHEURWEGHS, G. *Nicholas Udall's Roister Doister,* in *Materials for the Study of the Old English Drama,* New Series, Sixteenth Volume. Louvain: Ch. Uystpruyst, 1939. Scheurweghs imitates faithfully the Eton text, compiles many contemporary records, and analyzes the play exhaustively.

SHAABER, M. A. "The Meaning of the Imprint in Early Printed Books," *Library* s 4 XXIV (Je. 1943-Mr. 1944), 120-41. A classic study of what printers of the sixteenth century meant in their title pages and colophons.

SMYTH, C. H. *Cranmer and the Reformation under Edward VI.* Cambridge: Cambridge University Press, 1926. A clear account of a puzzling character and his problems in an age clouded with religious controversy.

TOULMIN-SMITH, LUCY. *The Itinerary of John Leland.* 5 vols. London: G. Bell, 1907-1910. The face of early Tudor England as seen through the eyes of a learned observer.

WATSON, FOSTER. *Vives: On Education.* Cambridge: Cambridge University Press, 1913. This translation, well-known to students of education, contains implications of interest to students of Tudor literature.

WITHINGTON, ROBERT. "Braggart, Vice and the Devil: A Note on the Development of Comic Characters in the Early English Drama," *Speculum* XI (1936), 124-29.

Index

DATE DUE

GAYLORD

PRINTED IN U.S.A.